A simple truth is that time is the most important factor in education. Time spent in engaged learning, in and out of school. Yet much time is wasted for our students, during the school day, with rote drills and abstractions, and during summers, when most students cannot afford the sports, camps, travel, and art lessons common in more affluent families. PUEO is an outstanding example of how Punahou, one of our nation's most impressive independent schools, has closed the "time gap" for public school students, providing them with amazing resources, teachers, facilities, equipment, and experiences.

In A Success Story in Public Education, Dr. Carl Ackerman, one of PUEO's founders, tells the inside story of how it led a private school to serve a larger public purpose, a model that has spread to independent schools across the country. One of its secrets is the power of one-to-one conversations and relationship-building, the Partnership-Marriage. Carl's own vision, enthusiasm, and humor attracted many partners and "spouses", and I'm honored to have been one of them.

Dr. Milton Chen
Senior Fellow, George Lucas Educational Foundation
Trustee, W. K. Kellogg Foundation

Palmetto Publishing Group
Charleston, SC

A Success Story in Public Education: The Clarence T. C. Ching PUEO Program at Punahou

First Edition

Printed in the United States

Paperback: 978-1-64990-519-2
eBook: 978-1-64990-511-6

Members of the Clarence T. C. Ching PUEO Program
on a one-day tour of the art museum

This book is dedicated to the students and faculty of the Clarence T. C. Ching PUEO Program at Punahou and to all who made this program possible.

It is also for my immediate family: my wife, Dr. Lyn Kajiwara Ackerman, and my daughters, Professor Laura Keiko Gilah Ackerman and Ms. Jennifer Xin Ackerman—all of whom spent years working in PUEO and supporting their husband and dad.

And finally, for my mother, as without the matriarchal guidance of Mrs. Leslie Rogers Steinmetz, this book would not have been possible. She guided all of her children, and grandchildren, into lives devoted to social justice.

CONTENTS

FORWARD

As the title of this book suggests, this is a story of a successful educational program called the Clarence T. C. Ching Partnerships in Unlimited Educational Opportunities Program, or PUEO (an acronym and the name of our Hawaiian owl). The PUEO Program's mission was to make sure public school students entering PUEO would graduate from high school and go on to college. Over seven years, PUEO gave students fine classes in the summer months after students completed their fifth grade at public schools in Hawai'i, and when students entered high school, the program offered credit-bearing classes followed by college prep classes. In a follow-up eighth year while students were in their senior year of high school, there were other activities which included eight to ten visits by a PUEO college counselor. All PUEO students had exciting academic activities during the school year. Still, this book is not a recounting of the PUEO Program; instead aspects of the program are presented in a series of vignettes that perhaps will best illustrate how this program got started, the problems it faced, and the heroic efforts of the many people that made the program possible.

Yet the history of PUEO also represents a unique business style, which I refer to as the Partnership-Marriage (P-M) style of business. While others refer to twenty-first century skills and "group models" in education, ours was much akin to the courtship model in partnering and then the more structured relationship of marriage. In terms of idea formulation and its implementation, P-M is highly successful. Often the director of PUEO would meet with one critical person, establish and discuss a good idea, and then implement this idea with the help of the partner and with the many hands paddling the canoe. In group models, often there is fine discussion, but the privacy of one-on-one conversations and the ability to build trust, inspiration, and ultimate success is stronger in the P-M model. So I hope this book is not only the catalyst that will help others make education in Hawai'i, the United States, and internationally a successful journey, but also will inspire others in non-educational fields to create the Partnership-Marriage model.

It is customary in Hawai'i to use the metaphor of the traditional Hawaiian voyaging canoe and the many hands that make the journey of this vessel possible. And indeed this is true of the Clarence T. C. Ching PUEO Program at Punahou School, too. Many hands. Many wise words of advice. Many people paddled in the PUEO Canoe. I want to thank them all.

Carl Rogers Ackerman—August 10, 2020

PREFACE

All but one of the chapters below begin with a question (something historians do when they begin to approach a subject), and then after the question in parentheses is a message about the subject of the chapter. Alexander Ivanovich Herzen, a nineteenth-century Russian intellectual who this author knew well only after two decades of writing a dissertation about him, advocated the use of parenthetical comments because anything is fair game within these unstructured "walls." I follow Herzen's lead here. Again, these chapters, in many ways, can be read separately, as the narration is in a storytelling style. In addition, as this book is built as a model for how to create a program, as each chapter is read, one can be guided into creating a system of one's own making or at least asking the questions that will lead to a program being built based on the Partnership-Marriage methodology.

CHAPTER I

Why was the PUEO Program Necessary? (The Big Educational Divide)

Several years ago, I was called into federal jury duty in downtown Honolulu. It seems that all jury-driven courtrooms exist in some central, downtown location, and this was true of my federal jury. Waiting on the steps of the courthouse for the building to open in downtown Honolulu, I looked at the many faces of those I suspected would be my fellow jurors. And indeed, once we got in and presented our summons, many of them were my suggested comrades (by training I am a PhD in Russian history, so please excuse this nomenclature). We all entered the courtroom slowly and, having been directed to an elevator that was too small to hold all of us, we took turns going up. We waited in an entry level room where a courthouse clerk gave us instructions about the day, and we all seemed to be eager to get going despite the pall-like silence created by our collective mission, our personal doubt, and almost everyone's inclination to play with the almighty cell phone.

Well, once we arrived in the courtroom, our distinguished judge went through the process of picking jurors. Our case was one about a man who was accused of sending illicit drugs through the mail on the Big Island of Hawai'i. He sat next to his lawyer, nervously turning around at various moments. He was tattooed, hair a bit messy, thin, Polynesian, and very nervous. I immediately wondered why he was in this circumstance—and I would never know about his relative guilt, if any, as I did not get picked for the jury.

Ironically, on that very day I had been invited to speak to students at the John A. Burns School of Medicine about the Clarence T. C. Ching PUEO Program, and the J.A.B. School was not far from the federal courthouse; I returned to this downtown Honolulu location in the evening after having taught some afternoon classes at Punahou School, as my jury role encounter and the federal court system had taken place in the morning. The medical students were all sitting politely in a semicircle in a classroom in the medical school, and the ubiquitous Matthew Nagato, the filmmaker who had included PUEO in one of his vignettes in his much-celebrated documentary *Ike*, was preparing to show his film. The students were all in informal garb and had the shiny, young faces of those who had succeeded in the educational system, both private and public. They had arranged for a potluck with food near the open arch of their semicircle of chairs. After the showing of *Ike*, the students, a good cross section of Hawai'i—Polynesian, Asian, and a few *haoles*—were quick with their questions and terrific with their comments. These young almost-doctors knew their future was secure—they were the cream of our educational institutions. Upper middle class status was only a few years away.

As I drove home to my house in the lovely Mānoa Valley in Honolulu, I began to think about this uneven experience during my day. On the one hand, I had seen what happens to an individual who might end up in our prison system, and on the other, the success written all over the young adults who spoke with self-assured future status and job security.

All the data about educational institutions in the United States point to low prospects for those who do not finish high school and even for some of those who do but fail to enter some sort of higher learning after high school. Also, there is universally accepted data about higher prospects and definitely higher income for those who finish some form of higher education. While I did not know the man who was on trial and I do not know the future of those medical students, they indeed did represent, on a very personal level, the educational divide in Hawai'i and the United States.

This book, in one sense, represents more hope for the educational institutions in our country through one program and one small group of dedicated people. It also underscores that public education at times (but not always) simply needs a small bit of help. Public education can prove very successful if our attention is laser-focused on the children.

The story of the Clarence T. C. Ching PUEO Program unfolds below, not in any chronological order, but within the context of vignettes that may help all who read this book, in education or not, who believe in the ability of one-on-one conversations to create systematic change. To create this change, one needs time, patience, and the willingness never to cast blame, but only to admire success and to constantly improve upon this success.

CHAPTER II

What was the Impetus for PUEO? (A Personal Vignette)

Years ago, I listened to the remarkable erudition of David McCullough, Sr., the noted historian and father of one of my friends at the Punahou School in Honolulu, Hawai'i. Yes, this is the school that graduated President Barack Obama (known as Barry when he was at Punahou). McCullough suggested that there is no such thing as a self-made man or woman. In a speech at Punahou School, he commented that we all receive help from many people—and so "self-made" is really not an appropriate term.

In that regard, the spark that started the PUEO Program perhaps came a generation earlier when my father and uncle lost both parents and were sent to live with an elderly aunt and uncle in New York City. Being unable to cope with the youngsters, their aunt and uncle sent the boys to what is now called the Governor's Academy in Massachusetts. This wonderful boarding school led these boys, Leopold and Lester, to attend Harvard (my father) and M.I.T. (my uncle). Dad went on to fly DC-3s in all arenas of World War II, with the most harrowing trips flying over the Hump—that is, over the Himalayas on the Burma route into China. He did many things after the war—almost all successful—ranging from newspaper writing to advertising and finally became a developer (with an unsuccessful run for governor in Arizona in 1960). I knew all these stories at a young age and realized the power of a private school education.

Leopold Ackerman running for governor in 1960 with presidential candidate John F. Kennedy

My mother, a Vassar graduate and New Yorker, settled with my father in Phoenix after World War II and started an integrated preschool in the 1950s in Phoenix. This was not easy. Once, my father, when he had launched his political career, was told by some heavyweights in the political scene in Arizona that he would need to tell my mother to stop her civil rights activities. To my father's credit, he replied curtly to this advice: "My wife is a Vassar graduate. I do not tell her anything."

Marrying three men at different times, each, as she says, "for the perfect time in her life," my mother was Gloria Steinem before the 1970s. Taking her children to anti-Vietnam War rallies, raising four kids in Phoenix, moving just north of Los Angeles to Malibu, and always maintaining a strong sense of loyalty to friends and a liberal-left ideology, this five-foot, two-inch Jewish woman dominated the academic, moral, and intellectual development of her children. The oldest and brightest child, Mary, went to UC Berkeley during the sixties, meeting Janis Joplin, Jimi Hendrix, and others when she was the girlfriend of the road manager for Country Joe and the Fish. The next child, Byron, was brilliant in mathematics as a graduate of Santa Monica High School (Malibu did not have a high school then). He was an anti-war activist, graduated from UCLA after years at Berkeley and Columbia, and became a noted computer specialist. Years during college were spent around the country organizing anti-war demonstrations, and as a leader of this movement, Byron gave a tour of New York City to John Lennon and Yoko Ono during their Bed-In period. The youngest in the family, Elizabeth Leslie (the second name after my mother), graduated from UC Santa Cruz after being a surfer, thoughtful and creative student, and always a great support to her friends and family. While employed in various administrative educational jobs in LA including a VP stint at Hamilton and Beverley High Schools, Tootie (her brother Carl nicknamed her this as he could not pronounce Elizabeth at an early age) recently started the Girls Academic Leadership Academy (GALA) in Los Angeles, the first all-girls public school in California for at least a century. She married the late Joe Hicks, civil rights activist and at one time CEO of the Southern Christian Leadership Conference in Los Angeles (SCLC was first started by Dr. Martin Luther King, Jr.).

Leslie Steinmetz (née Ackerman) with granddaughters. Front row: Jennifer Ackerman, Katarina Hicks, Megan Dervin-Ackerman. Back row: Natasha Hicks and Jessica Dervin-Ackerman. Missing: Laura Keiko Gilah Ackerman who will appear later.

This was my immediate family, and all were dedicated, devoted, and a bit uncompromising in their missions—but only because their missions were guided by altruism and a deep sense of social justice (and I did not even mention my two wonderful stepfathers, Fred Steinmetz and Jerome Shore, who were both at one time political activists also). Not to mention my stepmother, Celia Franco Ackerman, who, being of both Spanish-Mexican and Anglo heritages, had to avoid the rocks of other children who did not like this mixed race child in the small town of Miami, Arizona. She gained great fame in Phoenix by wearing mink in her pickup truck, all the while taking care of six children in the large adobe house near Camelback Mountain where I spent my summers. Celia had us all go to Catholic Mass (a rather interesting and wonderful experience even for this Jewish child). My half-brothers, Doug and Paul, shared the Ackerman name as they were adopted by my father. They taught me how to take care of those younger than I and were fiercely loyal to me as a younger brother, and they remain so to this day. Celia's sister and brother-in-law would often accompany us to ASU football games, and I remember my cousins Steve, Stacey, Stanley, and Alan (the Sanchez Family), and Uncle "Juke" and his wife, Auntie Deenie all rooting for the Sun Devils with us at Arizona State. As one of those serendipitous moments in life, my oldest daughter Laura just took an assistant professor job at ASU with her dashing husband Kyle, and my youngest daughter, Jennifer, will attend ASU as an undergraduate in the fall of 2020. More Sun Devil football games for sure. Of course, the point here is not on football, but my exposure to various ideas and concepts that ran the gamut of the American experience and also included the diversity of relationships and experiences that make our family—and our country—so wonderful.

My own journey as the third child in the original set of four took me from Phoenix (where my parents first settled), to Malibu (where my mother took up shop after the divorce), to Santa Monica (where I went to high school). This high school was the perfect microcosm of American society at the time with low-income students (below Montana St.), middle-income and upper- income students (above Montana St.), the upper-income students from Malibu, and the polyethnic and racial groups who attended this salad bowl school. We had a Black Student Union Club run by my friend Thomas Jefferson, a MECHA Club headed by another friend, Manual Alas, and many other clubs devoted to our multiracial and multi-interest student population. Several of us even started a tutoring program at a nearby elementary school, Broadway Elementary School on Lincoln Blvd. (where my mother taught), which, at that time, was in a gang-dominated area of Venice, California.

From Santa Monica High School (and a surreal camping trip in a VW Camper to the former Soviet Union, circa 1969, with my mother, Tootie and stepfather Fred Steinmetz, from Leningrad to Sochi, and a brief stint as an au pair in the Malibu Colony), I headed toward Berkeley. Being part of this radical campus, majoring in history, and being influenced by many left-wing groups allowed me to journey to Cuba with the Venceremos Brigade where I built apartments for several months (the name means "we shall overcome"). Seeing the goose-stepping Cuban army and hearing the speech in Jose Marti Square, Fidel Castro shouting, "Patria o muerte" (fatherland or death), made me reconsider the Left and drift toward more practical solutions. In addition, during my years in Berkeley several friends influenced me greatly: Andy Winfrey, Bonnie Smith, and Terry Kane Chinn (now Terry Moore). Andy let me know that it was possible to buy a house, even if one had to reach out to gather many different resources and in turn pay the mortgage by recruiting renters, in addition to introducing me to jazz music of all varieties. Bonnie showed me how to raise two children as a single mother while working full time and how to always be kind even in the most difficult circumstances. Terry revealed how to live one's life as an artist (as a bit of an eccentric) while maintaining life in the regular academic world. They were my partners in life at Berkeley.

Several years later, after my BA in history and two teaching credentials, I became a teacher at Saint David's Elementary School in

Richmond, California. Richmond at that time represented an area in California that had dire poverty; I learned a great deal from the Sisters of Notre Dame that ran this small school. My partner there was Barbara Kringle, a devoted and bright lay teacher.

While at St. David's, I received a call about an interview at UC Berkeley for a school called Iolani that was located somewhere in Hawai'i. Actually, while not being able to pronounce the name for a while, I was intrigued by Headmaster (and Episcopal minister) David Coon and his Assistant Head Charlie Proctor when I first met them at the placement center at Berkeley. My history training as an undergraduate had been good at Berkeley, and I could coach baseball, I told Headmaster Coon and Charlie, as I had played for many years as a boy. Iolani School sounded wonderful, and it was! I was off to Hawai'i, even though my family had a special intervention dinner with me in San Francisco to persuade me to think about the consequences of this decision. Hawai'i seemed awfully far away for my relatives—and they knew my proclivity for adventure.

Still, before I had left the Bay Area, I had taken two jobs. One was a paid summer internship with the Department of Labor that lasted for three years where I monitored the Summer Youth Employment Program under the Comprehensive Employment Act of Congress. This job allowed me to see PUEO-like summer programs all over the western region of the United States. My fiscal and programmatic monitoring took me all over California, Arizona, and Nevada. My mentor, Eric Gray, and I had long discussions about our work and the most efficient way to help kids get out of poverty. In addition, another mentor in another job at the Mission YMCA, Sandy Gong, helped me understand the plight of kids in the Outer Mission of San Francisco. We even took these fine kids camping (despite the wolves). Even today I remain an advocate for the Y and have remained on the board of our University of Hawai'i Y for the past twenty years or so.

Iolani turned out to be even better than I expected. The students were top grade, and the faculty was the same. A math teacher there, David Masunaga, was perhaps the brightest individual I had come across in my life, with his equations, Escher designs, mastery of many subjects, and even Russian language in the mix. Christopher Strawn, another faculty scholar, was the classicist extraordinaire who had a job in the music industry before he donned his Iolani Latin prowess. Chris could play Vivaldi while quoting Dylan or Prince. And finally, there was Alan Suemori, a gentleman who wrote plays at Columbia, and became both well respected and honored at Iolani. It was Alan who first introduced me to the book, Money Ball---so critical for the success of PUEO. Many years later at Iolani, my longtime friend and fellow teacher at Punahou, Dr. Bonnie Traymore, would teach Advanced Placement US History and work in a program similar to PUEO called KA'I. For the past twenty years or so, Bonnie became someone I called when seeking advice. This New Jersey turned Hawai'i resident gave great counsel and was a trusted friend, and both my daughters loved Auntie Bonnie. All of these critical relationships were met one-on-one; each proved to be not only a help in building PUEO, but in my overall living experience—these were the first Partnership-Marriage relationships besides the most important one with my wife, Dr. Lyn Kajiwara Ackerman, who I met at Iolani. Lyn has given me advice and has been my married partner for over thirty years.

Iolani's influence was profound, and its concept of "one team" was integral to the later development of PUEO at Punahou School. Started by Father Bray, a famous minister and football coach in Iolani's history, all actions at this school were directed toward the team. Headmaster Coon reinforced this adage by his direct and fair approach; the faculty as a whole and by specific high school class often met with Assistant Headmaster Proctor to discuss students' needs in a group setting. Teachers would discuss these students, and then Charlie would often write a letter to the parents, making corrective suggestions or simply applauding a student's actions. Focusing on cohorts of students and discussing them at large inspired the future cohort building blocks of PUEO. Also, it was legendary Iolani football coach Eddie Hamada who taught me to never give up on any student.

In addition to Iolani, the book *Money Ball*, chronicling general manager Billy Beane's approach to baseball, also inspired critical ingredients in PUEO and the P-M methodology. His approach was to hire baseball players, not on the basis of who looked like a good player, but by the statistical metrics of the player. Beane did not want the baseball player because of his looks—he wanted to see his on-base percentages. Beane turned to a trusted Harvard programmer as his key Partnership-Marriage relationship.

So I decided to copy the general manager of the Oakland A's by recruiting students to our program by going after the students in the great middle academically in the Department of Education (DOE)—the students who often were ignored and did not have their skills honed to become "the best." I knew that the gifted and talented students in the DOE in Hawai'i were already on-base and that the bottom 20 percent of students had many federal programs helping them already. I figured we could push these middle students to have great on-base percentages—which for me meant something akin to winning a World Series, having kids graduate from high school and enter into college. Still, I needed my "Billy Beane programmer," and I found her in the DOE as a midlevel Department of Education administrator named Colleen Murakami. She was the one who provided access to DOE schools, recruitment and access to the so-important DOE principals. Our Partnership began before the beginning of PUEO when I went into the DOE on a Punahou School sabbatical setting up service-learning programs across the Hawaiian islands. Our metaphorical marriage took place during years of deciding which classes would be suitable for PUEO, especially when our program grew into a seven-year program. All of us in PUEO relied on Colleen for DOE credit for classes (so critical for our success), information about getting material to school registrars, and for establishing our long-term memorandum of understanding with the Department of Education in Hawai'i. The individual P-M with Colleen Murakamai was so critical in accomplishing all these tasks.

On a final note, and somewhat unrelated except from the notion of a true grit perspective, I had great confidence in our success, as I had seen educational reform in Russia firsthand in the first days of the Mikhail Gorbachev regime (1986). Trained as a historian of Russia, I had been assigned to Special School 238 in Leningrad as an English teacher during the last days of the Soviet Union. With Glasnost and Perestroika on everyone's minds, the traditional thick journals of the nineteenth century replaced old stories about Lenin and Stalin. There was a quiet determination among the Russian people to get at the truth.

Just after my teaching stint at St. David's in Richmond, California, I was back in Russia with a group of high school seniors, and we witnessed the coup in Moscow on August 19, 1991. The Soviet Union collapsed, and so did many of the Marxist-Leninist beliefs. While currently Vladimir Putin is restoring many of the autocratic measures of the previous tsars and communist commissars, this does not discourage me in the long run—I had personally seen revolutionary change. New methodologies replaced old ones. Change was possible. Success was possible.

To end this chapter within the confines of the overall message by David McCullough, Sr., I am suggesting my parents and family (especially the ongoing advice of my wife) set the stage for social activism; individual partnership in Berkeley and at Iolani allowed for great learning to take place; *Money Ball* and Colleen Murakami allowed the Partnership-Marriage methodology to come into being. At Punahou School under the leadership of President James Scott, PUEO would get its start. The Gorbachev adventure let me know that anything was possible! The ideas so critical for PUEO's beginning were multifaceted and took place over many years.

CHAPTER III

How to Get Started? (The Partnering-Marriage/P-M Begins)

Interacting with the president of Punahou School had always been enjoyable. Dr. James Kapae'alli Scott had come back to Hawai'i to take over the reins of Punahou School in Honolulu after his undergraduate years at Stanford and doctoral studies at Harvard. Born into a modest family from Waimanalo, this *hapa* (multiethnic) young man was at Punahou from kindergarten through twelfth grade and raised locally in Hawai'i. Heralded as the first "Hawaiian" president of Punahou, he stepped up to the office following the very successful one of Dr. Roderick McPhee. Dr. Jim Scott was looking to make his mark.

As the "School on the Hill," so to speak, Punahou School was regarded in the community as the "rich *haole* school." Jim wanted to break this stereotype because not only had he been a scholarship student, but also his vision was to make Punahou a school that was truly racially and economically inclusive. So in some sense, the die was already cast for some sort of change. It is noteworthy also that Jim had been head of a school in Portland, Oregon, at the Catlin Gabel School where he had started a Summerbridge Program. This program took economically challenged kids in middle school from the Portland area and gave them three summers of tutoring at Catlin Gabel. The hope was to make the kids college ready.

When Dr. Scott arrived at Punahou and after several conversations about Summerbridge that I initiated, he indicated to me that he would like to start a Summerbridge type of program at Punahou. Without this desire, PUEO would most likely not have been created, or perhaps if it had been created, it would have been only with enormous difficulty. You need the support of the CEO, directly or indirectly, for a project of this magnitude. But—and this is a key "but"—his Summerbridge Program in Oregon eventually failed, primarily because of differences between the summer school director at Catlin Gabel and the Summerbridge director; so the structure of PUEO at Punahou needed to be much more carefully designed. Also, and most importantly, were the trustees at Punahou ready for such a new program, a program that was not focused on Punahou students? This was a critical question Jim had to manage.

Jim supported the idea of a Summerbridge-type program at Punahou as he himself had been a scholarship student from Waimanalo; he understood that income did not dictate interest, intellectual curiosity, or hard work. A scholarship student himself at Punahou, Jim went on to Stanford and then completed doctoral graduate work at Harvard. In a sense, his promotion of PUEO was the validation of his own education and his promise to pay it forward.

Jim is a man of Jewish, Hawaiian, Chinese, and other ethnic background (we call this chop suey ancestry in Hawai'i), speaks in a low baritone voice, and never speaks unless he has considered his words. This was the leading personality that appeared to both myself and the Punahou family. A man above six feet, a champion athlete at Punahou, including a celebrated pitching stint on the Punahou baseball team coached by the famous Eldredge brothers, Jim has a big frame and a smile to match. This president of Punahou sharing in the vision that would become PUEO was more than half the battle. Here was a critical Partnership-Marriage that began with the initial idea being discussed over several years (Partnership), and it was followed with twenty years of private meetings, often assisted by the magnanimous duo of Jim's administrative assistants, Audrey Seki and Sybil Saito, that were productive and sometimes quite intense (Marriage). The next issue was how to set up a program like Summerbridge, not only at Punahou, but within the communities that made up Hawai'i.

The first step, although we did not know it at the time, was a sabbatical for me during the 2000 school year, during which Punahou paid my salary for the semester and the Hawai'i DOE gave me an office at McKinley High School that I used as a base for my plan to set up service-learning programs across the state. McKinley is centrally located in Honolulu, as beautiful a public school as is possible, with long corridors of land and trees supported by multistoried buildings. Its administration building has photographs of well known graduates like Senator Daniel Inouye adorning its walls. In the math department's lounge in the administration building on the second floor, I had a small office. A wonderfully kind math teacher, Lynette Tom, turned out to be my guide and proponent during my one semester stay at McKinley.

My schedule, assisted by Mrs. Tom, consisted of traveling to schools across O'ahu and the outer islands and talking to teachers about service-learning (community service that is deeply attached to the curriculum with a substantial reflective piece). Judy McCoy, a midlevel administrator stationed out of Kaimuki Middle School, several miles from McKinley, was my boss, and I would have regular meetings with her during the semester. I was awarded an official DOE badge and made my way to the offices of school principals (protocol in the DOE) across the state before I gave my service-learning talks. Two of the most memorable stories took place on the islands of Lana'i and Kaua'i. On the former, which was owned largely by David Murdock (an early associate of my father in Arizona) at the time, a teacher at Lana'i High School was answering student questions, discussing a child with a parent, and fielding office messages when I arrived. This let me know what the norm for teachers was like at Lana'i High School. She spoke to me about service-learning from 4:00 to 5:00 p.m. "Dedicated" doesn't even cover a description of this teacher. The other episode that remains poignant was my discussion with the entire faculty at Kaua'i High School; here I gave a speech to teachers after school. I never knew if I had a made an impression, but several years later I learned that through a service-learning project, teachers and students from this high school had made a monument to the singer Israel "Iz" Kamakawiwo'ole, (whose music was celebrated through his song "Over the Rainbow" at the 2020 New Year's celebration in Times Square) at the Lihue Airport. Success.

This service-learning work led to a whole lot of trust in me on the part of DOE administrators, teachers, and staff members. At Kaimuki Middle School and at McKinley, I became a familiar face, and when my sabbatical came to an end, I had become friendly with a woman, a science resource teacher in the DOE, who would also be soon the head of service-learning, Colleen Murakami (mentioned earlier). Colleen became a major player in PUEO as she was the one who shepherded our credits through the DOE. She was indispensable for the success of the PUEO Program.

Colleen Murakami, a woman of great wisdom and a determination that is unmatched by anyone I have ever encountered, was one of the essential PUEO colleagues. She suggested classes for our high school students that would earn high school credit, such as Hawaiian History, Participation in Democracy, Performing Arts, etc. After a student completed the seven-year PUEO program, he/she earned up to six high school credits, and we even added two more electives to the mix. So, eight .5

credits were available to our students—this allowed PUEO students to take accelerated classes (AP, etc.) and the possibility to graduate early. Colleen knew how to usher these credits through the DOE so that each high school principal could approve of them and the registrars could add them to each child's transcript. We all knew PUEO was successful when we saw "PUEO at Punahou" on an official DOE transcript. Without Colleen, the quiet and effective midlevel DOE administrator, we would not have been able do so much in such a small amount of time. This initial Partnership with Colleen, which then broadened into a Marriage relationship taking place over nineteen years (from the time of my sabbatical) with thousands of one-on-one calls and hundreds of meetings, was so important to the Clarence T. C. PUEO Program at Punahou.

PUEO students gathered for an activity in Thurston Twigg-Smith Auditorium at Punahou

CHAPTER IV

Learning from Others on the Continent (Setting Up PUEO Through P-M)

Going back to that wonderful quote from the historian David McCullough, Sr., about no one being a self-made person—as all have received help—raised two significant questions for me: Why not see what others were doing in the same field in Hawai'i and on the mainland? Why not follow their lead?

So off on a plane I went with Dr. James Scott's blessing. First stop was University High School in San Francisco's Nob Hill district. The Julia Morgan-built school had the very first Summerbridge Program under the tutelage of the kind Meredith Laban; this was my first stop in discussing ideas for what would become PUEO. Summerbridge, which had a national following before it changed its name to the (national) Breakthrough Program that remains in existence today, aimed its efforts at middle school students. Most Breakthrough programs (and this was true of the initial Summerbridge Program I had discussed with Meredith) had three years of interaction with kids who came from poorer communities. Hiring college students and having a network of trainers, their summer courses focused on reading, writing, and mathematics, but they also had subjects particular to a given regional area. For example, in San Francisco, field trips would involve BART, trolley cars, and visits to museums, going on ferries in the San Francisco Bay, etc. By the end of three summers, students in Breakthrough—or so was the hope—would be better trained for their high school experiences, and the students would have college as their main goal. Walking into University High School, I was most impressed by Meredith's grasp of the challenges of her program and remembered her recruitment strategies: Meredith's limited staff would need to go to their SF partner public schools, make a presentation, and then leave recruitment forms with public school officials. This seemed both heroic and cumbersome. My initial partnering with Meredith did develop into the typical Partnership relationship, as we had several conversations in San Francisco and on the phone; she was always kind to me and a source of inspiration for many years to come (Marriage). Meredith's extensive career progressed to many different PUEO-like organizations, including now the Lorna Smith and Jose Oromi-led Horizons Program in schools across the United States.

My next stop was Head-Royce School in Oakland. I always feel a bit exhilarated crossing the San Francisco Bay Bridge (this was the older rendition of this bridge); there is something magical about looking at Oakland and Berkeley from San Francisco and looking at San Francisco from the East Bay. Head-Royce is located on the top of one of the many hills in Oakland, not too far from some forests and a nearby Mormon temple. You enter from the street and walk down to some very beautiful buildings and a pool that has a view of the San Francisco Bay. In one of the offices I visited was the wonderful Barbara Gee. Barbara has a quiet demeanor and a thoughtful approach to everything. She was and is a source of knowledge with her direct approach and her ability to answer all questions with a helpful comment. The Heads Up Program, which Barbara founded and developed, worked with students from the Oakland City School District.

Barbara's program started with kids in middle school and ran for four years. Kids attended Head-Royce summer classes, taking classes such as study skills, writing, mathematics, other STEM classes, and fine arts. Recreation and sports were in the afternoon for this one hundred-student program spread over four cohorts of twenty-five from entering sixth graders to entering ninth graders. Kids were all recruited from the Oakland public schools on the basis of applications completed, and all children were in the federal reduced/free lunch program (an indication, in most cases, of difficult economic circumstances for their families).

Barbara may not have been prepared for this large *haole* guy from Hawai'i (with gray hair—and I stand over six feet tall, and Barbara was closer to five feet tall), but when we discussed our respective missions and used Head-Royce as the model, she became my teacher. She saw me as an eager beaver who wanted to replicate many of her wonderful ideas. Our missions were similar, and she even handed over her budget. The budgeting process of Heads Up became a critical building block for PUEO (based on the wonderful accounting system set up by the adept Michele Morikami as a member of the PUEO team), and Barbara handed me a start in this process through this initial partnering relationship. After many, many meetings with Barbara (both in person on the phone and through email) and through a codirectorship in an organization called Private Schools with Public Purpose, which has now lasted for fifteen years and will be discussed later in these pages, we developed a solid business Marriage.

Barbara Gee and Carl Ackerman at the tenth PSPP in Washington, DC

Off I went to Seattle, Washington, and the Lakeside School. There I met a man whose warm countenance and hearty laughter, made me feel comfortable at once. T. J. Vassar was the director of the Lakeside Educational Enrichment Program (LEEP) at the Lakeside School. T. J. made me welcome rather quickly, and his generosity made a deep impression on me. I was particularly impressed by the fact that he took his LEEP students out on Seattle waterways and shepherded them through the exercises that fancy colleges leave for their crew teams. A special feature of LEEP was their Stand and Deliver Program, whereby students needed to present something about themselves or their families for five to ten minutes in front of the entire LEEP community. This was a very successful way to make the students bond with the program and to encourage eloquent public speaking. Teachers from LEEP worked tirelessly on these speeches with the kids. We in PUEO would integrate the "Stand and Deliver" part of the LEEP Program into PUEO, and we invited T.J. to come and speak for about a week to our faculty and students (through our chapels) at Punahou. So the message here is to borrow great ideas from others, and don't be afraid to have others come into your "home" to help encourage your program to grow. T. J. also introduced me to the wonderful Latasia Lanier, who he wanted to be his successor (and that is what happened). While the Vassar man has now passed on, his picture remained in my office during my tenure in PUEO, and he will always be an inspirational figure for PUEO. Quite frankly, I loved this man and what he stood for in Seattle and in life in general. In this case, the P-M relationship was so strong between T. J. and myself that it passed down to the younger generation, as represented by the most kind and sagacious Latasia.

Coming back to Punahou after these whirlwind visits, I still had to figure out how I was going to shape the program. After Dr. Scott, as the President of Punahou, announced in a faculty meeting in the fall semester of 2004 that I would be launching a Summerbridge-type program, the pressure was on! One answer to the beginning pressure came running toward me just after Dr. Scott's announcement in the form of my history colleague, Dr. John Bassford. John, an expert in Vietnamese history, had the perfect name for the program. Teaching Asian history (and other things at Punahou), John had brought over many people in his Vietnamese family and had them all live with him and his charming wife, Van Huong. I had the pleasure of teaching one of his two sons, and the other son is a science teacher still today at Punahou. John said, "Call the program Partnerships in Unlimited

Educational Opportunities—PUEO for short." Genius—and a fine example of how, if you listen and wait for a good idea, one will come from a friend (as in this case), an acquaintance, and even perhaps from a stranger. One should always strive to build Partnerships. Needless to say, PUEO (the name of the Hawaiian owl) became our name. This name had come from a one-on-one conversation in our high school academy quad after a typical faculty meeting. In this case, the P-M relationship had already taken place over more than a decade of history teaching, and the creation of the name came with this friendship and trust. So the P-M relationship can occur before great ideas are shared.

Well, my anxiety began to grow over one question: who was going to help me put PUEO together? The answer came over several months as Dr. Scott and I began to discuss possible candidates. Others in the Punahou community gave great suggestions. Eventually, after talking about and thinking about the very best fit for the new program, I submitted three wonderful names to Jim: Lon Wysard, former fifth grade teacher and now the assistant admissions officer at Punahou; James Kakos, then a new social studies teacher, who, after his stint in PUEO, became a dean at Punahou and now VP in our high school academy (with a focus on our huge athletic programs); and Kylee Mar, a trained librarian and archivist who had taken over the KEY Club (a service club) from me when I had gone on sabbatical. Good picks all. Lon worked on our curriculum, James would work on almost everything, but later specialized in our year-round events, and Kylee worked with me on recruitment and developing Hawaiian core values into the program. Within three years, Kylee had become the assistant director of PUEO.

You need a good team to get started, and mine had been suggested by many in the Punahou community—they were great. I established a separate Partnership with each of my three colleagues, and our

Marriage turned into the administrative body of the PUEO Program. I would also be remiss if I did not discuss the marvelous talents of our administrative assistant, Mrs. Seri Suzuki. As the program settled into existence after several years, Seri came on board and did everything from balancing our books to ordering supplies, including being an "auntie" to all in the program. Kind, overworked, and efficient, this woman often represented the heart of our program to anyone entering our office. Seri was, by training, a graphic artist—all of the graphic production that came out of the PUEO office looked truly beautiful. The team was complete.

CHAPTER V

How to Take Off? (PUEO starts in 2005)

On my suggestion, my team and I went to a Department of Education principals' meeting at the Hale Koa Hotel (the US Army hotel in Waikiki) during the 2004–2005 school year. It was there that we spoke to public school principals from the Roosevelt High School and McKinley High School complexes (complexes represent all the feeder elementary and middle schools that direct children into that high school—so many principals were present at this meeting). We drove from Punahou (in Mānoa Valley) about one mile to the Hale Koa with high hopes. It was the very beginning, and we were about to make the pitch for DOE students to be in our Punahou program. We decided to follow the models on the mainland and start with the middle school years. Still, the Department of Education principals were appropriately skeptical about Punahou School and its purposes (we have one large statewide school system in Hawai'i—our DOE). As one principal queried: "Is this a recruiting program for Punahou athletes?" We replied, "No," but at first this did not allay the feelings of those at the meeting—but we moved on. The DOE did permit us to recruit students, but only with a bit more help from our friend Colleen Murakami.

Of course, where to start with classes and structure? This was the question I posed to the masterful and creative mind of Dr. Brad Kerwin (at that time Punahou Summer School Director and now in charge of his own lucrative companies). Like with Colleen, this was one of the best examples of the Partnership-Marriage model. Brad was an expert in developing classes, testing, and an array of other educational pursuits—including his own business, The Reading Company. To get started, he wanted to put the initial class of PUEO kids (forty strong fifth grade graduates during the 2005 year) into two experiential classes: Robotics Lab—a class dedicated to creating robots with computers and LEGO—and Up, Up, and Away (the name taken from a television show about Superman)—a class dedicated to flight, including paper airplanes, motorized toy airplanes fueled by gas engines, and, eventually, rockets. These rockets were fueled with real rocket fuel and shot up thousands of feet from the Punahou middle field campus and came down, hopefully, on the same field through the use of small parachutes. Sometimes, when something went awry, these rockets became the property of various buildings on the Punahou campus. Perhaps they are up there still.

These were great first classes suggested by Brad (and other succeeding summer school directors from the most innovative Dr. Casey Agena, to Mark Hannington, to Dr. Todd Chow-Hoy, and to Jonathan Koshiba---all helped the PUEO Program), this Irish-descended loveable man who had grown up in southern California, where a rite of passage in his family was the surfboard and the ability to master the waves in his hometown of Hermosa Beach. Smiling and talking—almost always—Dr. K, as the kids would call him, had gone to Catholic schools in childhood, UCLA in his college years, and finally finished with a PhD in education from the University of Hawai'i. Brad was full of encouragement and treated every PUEO student as if he and Linda (his Delta Airlines flying, kind wife) were their parents. I often relied on Brad's advice for the program, including our field trips to various colleges for every child in the first two years of the program, building a culture of college here. Our many conversations over the years produced innovative classes and a firm foundation for all in PUEO.

In the afternoons in PUEO after the morning experiential classes, Brad and I, through the P-M model, decided to have a tutoring program for all the kids. We decided that older students should be teaching the younger kids. We recruited eight TAs; we called these TAs and other teachers using the Hawaiian word for teachers, *kumu*, and in our first year (2005), they were mostly seniors from Punahou School (and from my Advanced Placement European History course). Two of the initial teaching assistants who worked together teaching mathematics and English skills to ten PUEO students were Benjamin Washofsky and Laura Keiko Gilah Ackerman (my oldest daughter). Ben, a handsome but slightly disheveled and humorous young man, had a great rapport with the students. Laura, a superb student and a fine athlete, became devoted to the program—working for five years in PUEO. Each PUEO TA in the tutoring program was assigned five PUEO children (Scholars, as we would later call them). Ben and Laura decided to combine their flock. These ten kids were challenging, all coming from a poorer section of the windward side of O'ahu. Two kids in particular, post–fifth graders (the age students entered the PUEO Program) Joshua and Precious, always had a lot to say. Joshua, a child devoted to theater in vocation and in life, loved to make pronouncements in class; Precious, tall, talkative, and opinionated, was a good match for Joshua. Trying to keep class control over Precious and Joshua and others occupied every working moment for our two young *kumu* (TAs/teachers). Offering lessons in reading, writing, and mathematics each afternoon proved highly successful as Ben and Laura were college *kumu*: Ben headed towards the University of San Francisco, and Laura Keiko became a water polo-playing Claremont-McKenna student. Ben is now a principal of a school in the San Francisco Bay area, and Laura Keiko, along with dashing husband Kyle, has hung her shingle most recently at Arizona State as an assistant professor of organic chemistry. Of course, one would be remiss here to not point out that Laura's mother, Dr. Lyn Kajiwara Ackerman, worked with the third year PUEO students, teaching English, working with kids using computer games, and even taking our students on one of their international trips. Four girls were chosen to go to Vietnam with Dr. Lyn Ackerman. Laura's younger sister, Jennifer, worked the last two summers (2018-19) as a *kumu* in our drama program and continued in the summer of 2020 with an online teaching venue. PUEO became a family affair, and it worked. Of course, the P-M relationship occurred with all who worked in PUEO with their director (me), but what astounded me was the degree to which TAs went on to do such wonderful things after college—often with an educational bent, such as with Ben and Laura. Dr. Robert Witt, the longtime Director of the Hawai'i Association of Independent Schools, and who had been so helpful to me at PUEO's onset, had noticed this trend also.

Watching over these TAs (*kumu*) was one of the best teachers to grace a Punahou classroom, the second grade wizard Alan Lum. Besides playing basketball with President Obama when both were in high school, Alan's claim to fame was keeping all Punahou second graders interested in all that he did. His classroom was surrounded by chickens, crops, and art displays. So his presence around the standard academic curriculum made traditional education more like Summerhill or other educational innovative programs. Through mathematics, vocabulary lessons on the board, and in discussing their future college dreams, Laura Keiko and Ben were aided by Super-Teacher (S.T.) Lum. S. T. Lum had the advantage of years of teaching experience, which came in handy when wonderful students like Joshua and Precious made everything chaotic at times—as superior students are often wont to do. Alan taught the class Up, Up and Away in the morning. So shooting off rockets, playing in the real flight simulator (landing and crashing planes), and buzzing through gas-powered plane travel on our large middle field was also under the care of S. T. Lum. He simply loved the kids, and in turn they loved him. Laura and Ben would turn to Alan if the Precious/Joshua duo got too out of hand—much less the other children. S. T. Lum was always the critical chaperone (along with other teachers) on our many college visits (up to six in the first two years of the program). As director, I always felt assured that the children were well supervised off of campus, as S. T. Lum was with them.

Teaming these near-adult TAs with our young children provided critical examples of college-going individuals while allowing the PUEO children to have very playful and brother and sister-like teachers. After the first year of PUEO, all students wanted to come back. Precious would remain in PUEO for seven years, go on to an evangelical college outside of Boston, be elected student body president at this college, and have her fellow students raise enough money for her to return to Hawai'i in the summer. Joshua would graduate from high school and become a thespian for Disney World, and he came back one year to pay it forward by becoming a *kumu* in PUEO. One of their PUEO classmates, Kristy Huang, would enter Punahou School (10 percent of our PUEO kids would end up going to private schools in Hawai'i), and then she went on to Princeton on a Gates Millennium Scholarship. When we last heard from Kristy, she was working in an accounting firm on Wall Street. This firm apparently did some work in Washington, DC, trailing the exploits of a DC school system and pointing out some improprieties and, by doing so, helped heal a problematic school system. What comes around goes around—Kristy was paying it forward.

Of course, it is always good to hear about PUEO in a student's own words, and what follows is such a reflection by Kristy Huang about her experiences.

How PUEO Helped Me Get to College

By Kristy Huang

March 1, 2020

My parents always emphasized the importance of education and going to college when I was growing up. They immigrated to the United States at the tail end of the Vietnam War. Their childhoods focused more on survival than education, and, consequently, neither of them had the opportunity to finish high school. I took advantage of my parents' sacrifices and studied hard to make my American Dream story come true.

First-generation, low-income students face unique challenges in getting to college and then getting through college. My parents always pushing me to go to college removed one barrier, but they didn't know exactly what it would take to get there. PUEO helped me make college possible, from introducing me to the idea of college at a young age and reinforcing the fact that I would go to college year after year to helping me build my college and scholarship applications to actually get there.

What I did not understand as a fifth-grader (and probably didn't understand until I started my college applications), is that getting to college is more than just getting good grades, which is what my parents pushed me toward since they didn't understand the world of postsecondary education themselves. Looking back now that I've graduated from college, I am very grateful that PUEO broadened my perspective on education and exposed me to so much more. College and education are not just about how much you learn academically. PUEO gave me a more fun and holistic view of learning. From programming robot cars in RoboLab to building airplanes and rockets in Up, Up, & Away, I learned in a fun and creative way. I learned more about the culture and history of Hawai'i, the place I grew up in, through exploring fishponds and irrigation systems, pulling weeds in *lo'i* patches, visiting Iolani Palace, and chanting *olis*.

I've always been quiet and shy, which makes things like public speaking and developing relationships difficult. During our first few years, I had to do an *I Ku Wa*, where I would stand and deliver something about myself to my peers and *kumus*. I was terrified each time I had to get up and present. People probably couldn't hear my quiet voice sitting in the back, but slowly I got better at projecting, and presenting got easier over the years. Our magic class had us repeatedly practicing magic tricks in front of each other before performing at our final show. When we turned our play into a variety show within days of our performance in our performing arts class, I surprised myself by choosing to present a poem I had written instead of doing something with a group. I had the confidence and projection to fill Twigg-Smith Pavilion with my voice.

Throughout the years, I always had my fellow PUEO Scholars and *kumus* by my side every step of the way. Whereas the focus at home was on work, whether that meant schoolwork or translating for my parents or helping out with my parents' business, at

PUEO I learned not to take life so seriously, that there was more to life than getting good grades. I could always count on my *kumus* to show up each day with a smile, supporting us as we soaked in everything like sponges. I was surrounded by students who came from similar backgrounds as mine, and there was a shared understanding that PUEO was investing in us as students. Our teachers and principals saw our potential despite our families' socioeconomic status and where we came from.

This connection allowed me not to get bogged down by the part of my identity that I am reluctant to reveal. Rather, I could just be myself and work on figuring out who I was. While I am still reserved today, PUEO encouraged me to push the boundaries of my comfort zone, to present myself with more confidence, and to be comfortable being myself around people.

PUEO started bringing more nuanced ideas around "college" into my everyday conversations, which I lacked at home, by starting to take us on college tours from our very first summer in the program. We got to meet college representatives and students to tell us about college life, extracurricular activities, dorms, majors, and the different reasons they chose their particular school, such as small class sizes, study abroad programs, and how urban or rural the surrounding community is. All of this encouraged me to take a holistic view of college. These conversations continued every summer and during our various events during the school year. During our last summer, our PUEO college guide class helped us turn those conversations into actions. PUEO helped me to navigate the confusing and overwhelming college application process and offered guidance on my application, including my essays. I was able to have a solid draft of my 500-word common application essay completed the summer before my senior year of high school, giving me time to focus on scholarship applications in the fall. Even before college applications, we knocked SAT tests out of the way. While taking SAT prep was the norm for my classmates at Punahou, I did not think it was necessary as a first-generation student and did not even consider the expense as a low-income student. The SAT prep course we took the second to last summer boosted our preparation and confidence in a key component of college applications.

As the oldest of five children who are all in the program, I've already seen how PUEO has impacted my younger siblings as well. College has now become the expectation in my family. I try to provide as much support as I can to my siblings on their journey to get to and through college, but that is limited to my own personal experience and what I can communicate from the east coast. I appreciate that my siblings are able to receive the same level of support I did from PUEO.

Pictured below is Kristy Huang graduating from Princeton University in 2016. Standing with her is one of her former *kumus* and postgraduate student (also at Princeton) Dr. Laura K. G. Ackerman.

It would be prudent here to hear from another member of our first class of students, Precious Totten, who was mentioned earlier. Like Kristy, Precious gives her take, in her own words, on the PUEO Program:

February 2020
Aloha,
My name is Alena Precious Totten. I am from Kahalu'u, Hawai'i. I am a graduate of the PUEO Program, Class of 2012. I first entered the program in the summer of 2005. As a child, I always wanted to be a singer. I was very ignorant about what it meant to plan or even think about the future. The PUEO Program opened my eyes to possibilities of what my future could look like. I learned about career options, life skills, and the importance of higher education. Most of all, I gained knowledge of who I was capable of becoming.

Every summer, PUEO continually gave me building blocks for my future. Through the summers, I was educated in many different courses such as robotics, aeronautics, marine biology, Hawaiian history, economics, and more. Over the years I was not only being educated in all these different topics, but I had the opportunity to get ahead in my education. At a young age, these courses helped me to understand that learning can be exciting and beneficial in ways I had never known. I was introduced to higher education and career options from the very start. Every Friday we would take a field trip to a different college on the island of O'ahu. It was because of those field trips I had decided I wanted to become a prosecuting attorney. During a trip to the University of Hawai'i at Mānoa, I was intrigued by the conversations about career paths. I had spoken with a guide about what I was interested in, and she suggested I look into different professions in law and even encouraged me to look into the best law schools in the country. I went home that day daydreaming about wanting to become a lawyer and attending Brown University. As I continued in the program, I continued pursuing that specific career. PUEO supported my pursuit by supplying the necessary information and guidance.

When I was a junior in high school, I chose to change my choice of career due to new interests and experiences. I went from pursuing a career as a prosecuting attorney to pastoral ministries. PUEO provided resources for college and financial scholarships to aid my passion and interests in biblical studies. It was a great help when PUEO provided college counselors my senior year in high school to help guide me into my next step in life. They helped in strategizing options for my future in college and postgraduate life.

One of my favorite parts of the program was the *kumus* and TAs. They provided safety for me as a child. They provided a safe place for me to express my misunderstandings, excitement, fear, and joys about the future. They invested a lot of their time in class, as well as outside of class, to help me understand certain courses I needed extra help in. They taught me through their own experiences to be young but to also be wise. They supported and believed in who I could be. This instilled confidence, courage, and grit into my life that set me up for long-term success.

After I graduated from James B. Castle High School in 2012, I left Hawai'i to pursue an education in biblical studies in Haverhill, Massachusetts. I applied all that I had learned in PUEO to adapt and succeed in my undergraduate career. I graduated from Northpoint Bible College in the spring of 2016 with a BA in Biblical Studies with a double major in youth counseling. After graduation, I was blessed with a job opportunity at a church as a youth pastor. The church was located in Massachusetts where I received my ministerial license with the Assemblies of God. I continued to work with youth programs from 2016 until July of 2019. I lived in Massachusetts for a total of seven years and recently returned home to Hawai'i. I am currently working at Christian Academy as the events manager and employment administrator. I am continuously learning while doing what I love.

I am blessed to live a life of fullness and joy. I thank God for allowing great opportunities that changed my life for the best. The PUEO Program has been one of those incredible impacts. I know without this program I could not be where I am in life today. Thank you to the PUEO Program for teaching me that life has a numerous amount of opportunities. Thank you for caring about the youth of the future. Thank you for teaching me more necessary tools for life than I could have ever imagined. I pray that the PUEO Program will continue to be a Partnership of Unlimited Educational Opportunities, where the youth of tomorrow are supported and inspired to create a future of endless possibilities.

Mahalo Nui Loa,
Alena Precious Totten

Alena Precious Totten Graduating from Northpoint Bible College as Class President in 2016.

CHAPTER VI

How to Create Partnerships Using the P-M Methodology? (The Best of P-M)

PUEO was only as successful as the Partnerships we created in the community. Through our initial Partnerships and then our Marriages, we created a firm basis for all that we did across Hawai'i. In this chapter, I discuss how many P-Ms developed and how they helped us in our endeavors. In addition, by examining these Partnerships one can fully understand how the Clarence T. C. Ching PUEO Program at Punahou School developed and succeeded.

Coming to Hawai'i from Russia and his mother's side of the family from Wales, Fred Reppun became a second-generation doctor, first practicing in Moloka'i and then was a general practitioner on the windward side of O'ahu. Raising seven children, with the oldest being a girl, Martha, and the rest boys, Dr. Reppun ingrained hard work and a certain skeptical streak into all his children. Building a large and beautiful house in Kaneohe overlooking Kaneohe Bay, he started his children in public schools, but soon they made their way to Punahou. After degrees at Hamilton College, Harvard, and other fine institutions, Charlie, John, and Paul made their way back to Hawai'i as taro farmers, battling land developers for water rights and becoming very much a valued part of the Hawaiian community. Josh, the youngest son became a respected educator, and spent years at Punahou and other private schools.

The Reppuns' work on the windward side of O'ahu endeared them to all in that area. One community organization, the Kualoa-He'eia Ecumenical Youth Project (KEY Project) became of particular interest to John Reppun, the rugged former high school football player who befriended President James Scott (mentioned earlier) at Punahou School. John became the CEO of KEY, which had its focus on preserving the land, feeding the poor, and taking care of the elderly as just a few of the things that made up its mission. Of course, being located right next to Kahalu'u Elementary, a host of tutoring programs also made their way into KEY.

Our relationship with John led to ten students being recruited from the fifth grade at Kahalu'u Elementary School. While other schools nominated one, two, or three students, our Partnership with John and his family allowed for more students here. The Reppun brothers went to Punahou, many classes had used their taro farm as a way to expose Punahou students to the environment, and the AP European History class at Punahou often came out to help at the Thanksgiving fundraiser at KEY. John and I spent many an hour discussing the development of PUEO. This was a P-M relationship that was cemented by many years of working together and building a great deal of trust; it also was a P-M relationship that helped us recruit students in Kahalu'u where John and his brothers lived.

The way our recruitment worked in PUEO was that principals of schools (or teachers, counselors, etc.) would nominate the students on two criteria: (1) the great middle academically of the class—20th percentile to 80th percentile, and (2) all of the students had to be free or reduced lunch students according to US federal guidelines. After principals sent us the names of prospective students in August and September, Dr. Brad Kerwin and I would go out to each school (normally in October and November), meeting the students and inviting them to the opening admissions lu'au in the spring along with their families. Students then spent seven years with us in PUEO classes at Punahou School. Brad, a trained magician, often performed a magic trick at each school for the kids; in the latter years, when we had over twenty recruiting schools all across O'ahu, this recruitment process would take several weeks. Sometimes it would take us several hours just to get to a school near the north shore of O'ahu. Of course, Brad would charm all the elementary school officials by handing them his business card, which he initially lit on fire. Sparks would fly, and all people, in every office, would beg Brad for more magic tricks. The result of these recruiting trips would be forty to fifty more kids entering PUEO each year. By about 2018, we had over 330 kids in the program, with each of the seven cohorts having somewhere between forty and fifty kids. Every child was on a seven-year scholarship in the PUEO Program with a full year of college counseling and test preparation in the extended eighth year. This eighth year took place when the students were in their senior year of high school.

Back to the Partnership with the Reppuns. John Reppun, as a PUEO supervisor, waited at the bus stop (about forty-five minutes away from Punahou School on the other side of O'ahu) at KEY with the students as they departed in the morning about 5:30 a.m., and he also saw them, often with his wife Lynette, as they were dropped off at KEY each afternoon around 4:00 p.m. if the traffic was good—later, if not. He attended the opening lu'au and even housed some of our *kumu* at his abode—in particular two wild New Yorkers named Andrew and Ben. He and his college educated brothers talked to the kids about having a meaningful farming life. They often echoed the words of the folk singer Ry Cooder: "The farmer feeds us all." John was frequently in slippers or barefooted, and so were his brothers. T-shirts and jeans marked these men—or, if forced to dress up for a special occasion, an aloha shirt with jeans. These men of the earth represented a critical P-M for PUEO.

James Toyooka is the principal of Nu'uanu Elementary School. In many ways he represented our collective relationship with the principals in the Department of Education. Each principal (and at the end of my fifteen-year tenure in PUEO, this represented over eighty principals) had their very own P-M relationship with me. I would call James to set up our yearly appointment with our new recruits (he being with one of our original thirteen recruiting schools with PUEO and forty children the first year), and we would "talk story." Sometimes we would talk about his former business career, and I would talk about my life as a historian of Russia; at other times we would discuss students, our lives in education, and even our families. When Brad and I would get to Nu'uanu Elementary School off of the Pali Highway, sometimes getting lost, the student would be ready and an empty room would be available; James would generally greet us as we walked in the door. His staff was friendly, and Brad would hand out his "burning" magic business cards.

The level of professionalism on the part of James Toyooka was repeated by all the principals (and others) in the DOE, including, notably, Principal Derek Minakami at Kaneohe Elementary School, Stacy Miyashiro, counselor at Lanakila, Principal Kelly Bart at Likelike, Amy Arakaki and Naomi Matsuzaki at Kahalu'u Elementary School, Ron Okamura at McKinley High School, CAS (Complex Area Superintendent) Ann Mahi, Principal John Thatcher from Connections Charter School in Hilo, and the list continues ad infinitum. Sometimes I was invited to complex area meetings. Each high school in the DOE defined the complex, with middle schools feeding into the high school and their accompanying elementary schools all defined by this complex designation (i.e. Roosevelt High School defined the Roosevelt Complex). The principals were so kind to me, and they supported our work in PUEO. What a collective gift to Hawai'i—the DOE principal cadre and each, purposefully, with a special P-M relationship with me. As I mentioned earlier but bears repeating here, when I left PUEO during the summer of 2019, this represented over eighty P-M relationships with DOE principals.

Dr. Marlene Zeug constituted a special P-M, as she represented the YWCA at first and then was employed in the superintendent's office of the DOE a few years later. We met as Marlene was working for the YWCA as second in command. Her trusty surfboard was always in her office. At roughly a bit above five feet, Marlene was a former Division I college basketball star; this administrator at the YWCA was so impressive. She rebuilt Café Julia, a local favorite hotspot at the YWCA, working both as a planner and architect. Marlene worked in PUEO in our fifth year (P5 Program) where kids developed their own societies based on the US model; she then offered space in her Y for some of our PUEO students during our former Governor Linda Lingle's Furlough Friday Program that closed public schools on Fridays. Through all of this, Marlene and I were partners, often meeting for coffee at Starbucks or for lunch or dinner at Zippy's Restaurant (our local family restaurant in Honolulu with many locations). A turn in our Partnership, where the relationship matured to Marriage, was when Marlene started working for our superintendent of schools, the hardworking, adept, and results-producing Kathryn Matayoshi. Marlene, along with our ace in the hole Colleen Murakami, worked to get us our memorandum of understanding (two by the time I left PUEO) with the Hawai'i State DOE and helped us meet with the superintendent and her successor, the gregarious

Dr. Christina Kishimoto. Aided by Colleen and Marlene, we were also able to meet with Assistant Superintendent Katherine Kawaguchi and Assistant Superintendent Daniel Hamada, both of whom kindly and efficiently helped us get DOE credit for our high school PUEO classes.

Superintendent Matayoshi and I had wonderful meetings, almost always arranged by Marlene. Most recently, PUEO had a very productive meeting with Superintendent Kishimoto about our ability in PUEO to track all of our students in a Legacy List notebook. This notebook allowed us to see where our students were in college, and, after graduating from college, in the workforce. I had assigned two fine PUEO colleagues to complete this task—both able and hard working—Dr. Nicholas Perih and Mr. John Bickel. We offered this most powerful data-driven notebook as a way for the DOE to track all of its students. Marlene was indispensable in all of this and offered a remarkable example of our P-M types of relationship, especially ones that developed even as our partner changed jobs.

Dennis Suyeoka in the Atherton YMCA was another P-M example. This Partnership-Marriage proved very productive. Located a stone's throw from Punahou School was the Atherton YMCA. For over two decades I had been on the board of managers of this Y, but early on in the PUEO Program I realized that P7 students taking classes at the University of Hawai'i could be fed at the one-man-operated Coffeeline Café at the Atherton. Besides serving PUEO during the infamous Furlough Fridays (mentioned earlier), the Metropolitan Y had been one of three locations where we placed our PUEO students, not wanting them to stay at home during these "holidays." One must note here that our former governor Linda Lingle is a gracious, generous, and intellectually gifted individual. Still, this was not good policy from my perspective. But then again, I am sure she was trying to balance many things, including our state budget.

As the UH classes lasted often through the early afternoon, we needed to feed our cohorts of over forty students, their teachers, and

TAs in the P7 Program. Dennis was the answer. From lasagna to steak, from teriyaki chicken to *lau lau*, Dennis served our children in a gourmet chef way. Lunches were delicious, and the café surroundings most would call Berkeley-like—laid-back and hip! Dennis would serve the food for three of our five weeks of the summer program, and for the other two weeks our students would get a university food card—practice for their college years. As I walked around Coffeline, the kids were absorbed in conversation and quietly eating their delicious lunches. What began as a Partnership with Dennis became a Marriage full of lunches. What a delightful person. The P-M relationship with the Y extended to the head of the Atherton Board of Managers, Lesli Yogi, and to the President and CEO of the Y in Hawai'i, Michael Broderick. All of our younger students received free lunches through the remarkable kitchen manager at Punahou, Marcia Wright, who served us more than three hundred lunches daily in our cafeteria. Another internal P-M!

Youth Service Hawaii, formerly Teachers and Students at Work for Hawaii, is a service-learning nonprofit that several teachers, including myself, established in the 1990s. One key person from this organization who helped PUEO in many ways was Kamehameha teacher Judy Cramer. Judy Cramer came to and worked at many of our year-round functions in PUEO. Several times during the school year, we would have different student cohorts report to Punahou School on a Saturday in the fall or in the spring and attend classes sponsored by various organizations. The P-M relationship had already been established with Judy years before through Youth Service Hawaii, but her workshops on service-learning and the environment added such an organized touch, even with students rotating between her workshop and several other workshops provided by other nonprofits. She helped all communities in Hawai'i with her good friend, the most generous Ellen Schroeder, by always including students on a youth philanthropy board that actually gave out grants up to $1000 from YSH for service-learning projects. Judy is now the chief executive officer of YSH with family court judge Steven Nakashima as the president of her board of directors. Our P-M with Judy allowed our PUEO students to further their education about multiple environs in Hawai'i and about the significance of serving others. One could also mention here Mark Kalahele, a very successful businessman in the community, who, like Judy, joined us at various events and offered our students a keen insight into the making of the traditional Hawaiian canoe. Mark became a regular during our PUEO events in the school year. His uncle, Imai Kalahele, a well known poet in Hawai'i, had led a literature workshop during one of our first year-round activities. Two more fine P-Ms here.

Russell Motter, one of my closest friends in life and my colleague on the Atherton YMCA Board, also had a P-M relationship before he came to formally work for PUEO. We met initially at the University of Hawai'i in graduate school and then developed a great and close friendship over the years. Russell, as an in-house administrative analyst, gave me advice about the systems operating in PUEO. He explained how there was a wide differential between our mathematics students in our SAT classes (sixth year of PUEO, or, as we say, P6) during the summer. This information helped us get math tutoring during the summer when PUEO students needed help. He also worked with our longtime dean of students Tim Lucas and longtime PUEO counselor Matt Nakamura in reaching a consensus about tutoring during the summer in a place we eventually called "The Nest." What was the most helpful ingredient of Russell's tenure was his ability to make people laugh with his light countenance and his interjection of kind and humorous comments during our administrative meetings called PAT or PUEO Administrative Team. PAT consisted of administrative representatives from each cohort (P1–7) and a few other key people, including a representative from Punahou's development team and our various Punahou summer school directors (mentioned earlier). Russell, a tall, and friendly person, teaches at Punahou's sister school, Iolani. His favorite class at Iolani may be his African American history class, and his graduate work was on President Jimmy Carter. One cannot overestimate the laughter that Russell brought to our PUEO Administrative Team meetings, especially when the discussion got a bit too contentious—which was not often, but Russell had the cure. Russell held various administrative positions: Director at the YMCA, History Department Chair at Iolani School, and now he is the CEO of our local Elks Club in Honolulu. They call him the "Exalted Ruler" (perhaps in jest, but it is official).

Suzanne Sato was a P-M developed inside of Punahou School. She was in charge of foundation relations in support of Punahou, and one of her multiple charges was the Clarence T. C. Ching PUEO Program. Suzanne escorted donors into our activities from our opening lu'au for new students to our year-round activities, to our five-week summer program. In almost all cases, I would send out our younger *kumu* (TA teachers) to walk around PUEO with Suzanne and our potential and seasoned donors. I thought the program spoke for itself and was very comfortable with students talking about the program, and I was exceptionally proud of all of our TAs. Suzanne wrote all our donor reports. Part of our Partnership that really turned into a Marriage quite quickly was that she could call or email me at any time, and I would make the turnaround for whatever she requested within hours—always. Most of the time it was within minutes and, at most, two hours. Suzanne wrote beautifully, with illustrations and pictures in each report. She checked and rechecked names and numbers, and our donors always seemed pleased. Of all the people who worked for PUEO, it was Suzanne who advocated for PUEO with our donors. Her role on the PUEO

Administrative Team provided keen insight and often a moderating influence. Suzanne, an artistic and precise individual, was indispensable for the success of the PUEO Program.

Jonathan Clarke Sypert came to become the leader of the P6 drama program through an initial Partnership with one of the only professional theater groups in Hawai'i, the Honolulu Theater for Youth, or, as most of us call it, HTY. By sitting down with the CEO of HTY, Louise Lanzilotti, in Starbucks, Mānoa, with her educational director, Dan Kelin, at her side, we were able to produce the broad idea of students working in theater and dance in their sixth year of PUEO. In another meeting at the same locale, we were able to hire Jonathan Sypert and Kealoha Wong, two artists who really are artistic gifts to all in Hawai'i. In that initial summer of 2010, we began to produce student-driven productions centered around an array of societal issues such as drug addition, bullying, and gay relationships and expertly directed by Jonathan and Kealoha during that first year with their extraordinary expertise in dance and poetry, respectively. In subsequent years, Jonathan would rely on the expertise of the experienced DOE teacher, the magnanimous, kind and always-looking-young Sarah Kern. In 2019, we invited Bay Area artist Roger Dillahunty from his Berkeley studio, The Beat, into PUEO. During this time, my final summer, the performance produced by the PUEO P6 (sixth year) students was truly incredible and in many ways made them look like professional dancers and artists. Always on the second to last night of the PUEO summer program, the students would deliver their performance to parents, friends, and interested PUEO patrons. It was one of our favorite times in PUEO.

Carolee Nishi, hula instructor extraordinaire at the Nu'uanu YMCA, nominated students from her *hui* (group) to the PUEO group. She was only one of two people who was afforded the opportunity to do this (as this was not a school nomination process). A grandmother with a big heart and very strict, her girls and boys danced various forms of hula with poise and grace; some of the children played the ukulele and guitar to accompany their dances. Most of the time, Carolee, a petite and friendly lady, would also sing with various adult members of the *hui*. Her *hui* consisted of dancers whose ages ranged from three to eighty-three. Carolee would nominate public school children who fit our criteria (free or reduced lunch and in the great middle academically), but these students could enter at any P Level (1–7), which made them anywhere from ten to eighteen. She nominated four special boys from one family whose parents were not present but whose auntie had adopted them and gave them the love they all deserved.

This is a story in itself. The Maluyo boys live in a modest apartment in Honolulu. In his first year in the P3 part of the PUEO Program, the oldest, Mana, followed the usual plan of taking mathematics and English in the morning and magic in the afternoon. Mana (official name Darren) would continue on for four more years in the program, matriculating from McKinley High School and going on to Southern Virginia University, where he taught all there to call the cafeteria workers at the school "auntie" (something many Hawai'i kids do—that is, calling adults "auntie" and "uncle") or "uncle". He took his wonderful ukulele playing prowess with him—which he had learned, of course, from Auntie Carolee. By the time Mana left Honolulu for Southern Virginia, he was also an accomplished dancer of various forms of hula. As Mana was the oldest of four, his three younger brothers, Darryl, Dezmen, and Devon (the youngest sometimes called Mingo) also joined the program at the P1 level. Darryl, the second oldest, thrived in his P3 magic year, performing for his regular school and in other public arenas. The youngest two Maluyo brothers continue to thrive in the PUEO Program today.

One last interesting factoid about the oldest Maluyo, Mana, is that he was one of the four students chosen during his senior year in PUEO to take a trip to China under the sponsorship of Chris Choy and his Learning Across Borders group. While this was a type of science day competition in Beijing with educational travel attached, Mana stole everyone's hearts with his prowess on the ukulele. I remember receiving a note from a parent chaperone from Iolani School on the trip giving high praise to Mana. The power of the Partnership-Marriage arrangements, in this case with Carolee Nishi, often led to students entering the PUEO Program, and the trajectory of their lives, and that of their families, would change forever.

Matt Levi was the second of the non-principals who could nominate for the PUEO Program. His Lawakua Kajukenbo Club took kids from the projects and poorer areas around O'ahu and entered them in a rigorous regimen of Hawai'i-based martial arts. Matt, a five-foot-eight individual, the son of Holocaust survivors turned University of Hawai'i professors, who commands the respect of all from his gruff physical appearance, has a heart of gold. Each January and June, his students demonstrate their martial arts prowess in front of many leaders in the judicial, police, and educational communities. Matt sees this martial arts program as an alternative to juvenile incarceration and jail. His intervention in the kids' lives provides a real alternative to our criminal justice system. And this is not all—Matt makes sure that almost all of the private schools in Hawai'i provide scholarships for children, and he made it happen with PUEO with our P-M relationship. With great joy I would see our PUEO children perform their prowess twice a year in the LK Club under Matt's direction. Due to our P-M relationship with Matt Levi, a few students upon his nomination were accepted each year to the Clarence T. C. Ching PUEO Program. Matt defines the meaning of the word *mensch.*

Initially our Partnership with the Academy of Arts in Honolulu (front cover of this book) came through a teacher whose medium was in the metallic area, Dr. Bob Grossman. In the afternoons, our high school students could take this elective on the third floor of Bishop Hall at Punahou. Later this initial Partnership took off under the leadership of an enlightened administrator at the Academy, Vince Hazen. Vince took our students and provided great scholarships for all of them; again, our high school students could take art classes at the Academy of Arts, and he offered several classes: ceramics, painting, and metallurgy. Our students were bused to the Academy just after lunch and spent several hours each day with trained art teachers at this marvelous art center. The highlight for most of us was organizing a day during the academic year where our students took over the entire Academy of Arts in Honolulu. This was over two hundred kids in our P2–6 classes, and the classes included those offered during the summer with others added such as photography, Chinese calligraphy, and meditative charcoal drawing. What began as one class by one teacher led to Vince and I having many discussions at the more than lovely Art Museum Café, always paid for by the more than generous Vince. After Vince moved on to the Kamehameha Schools, a series of gregarious assistants who were previously directed by Vince took over. The Marriage continued.

Our students in their P7 year often would take classes at the University of Hawai'i. This was set up originally by the soft-spoken and powerful Dr. Amy Agbayani, who for years was and is the Democratic Party's quiet behind-the-scenes woman who made things happen and often got her party candidates elected. Amy often arranged space for our students and also arranged for our P6 students to get admission promises (if they had the grades and scores) to the University of Hawai'i once the students completed their sixth year in the program. Being on the UH campus during their last summer cemented the notion of college for our PUEO students. My Partnership with Amy began in the Coffeeline Café during the first years of the program and concluded with a Marriage based on so much trust that all it would take to get our students a room on the University of Hawai'i campus was a phone call.

The tall and brilliant Cheri Nakamura is the CEO of HE'E (Hawaiian for "octopus"), and the interlocking legs metaphor for this organization was perfect, as HE'E promotes DOE children through educational legislation and by advocating for DOE parents. The many legs of the HE'E octopus crossed over the complicated DOE terrain. I spent many a day in the HE'E office listening to a variety of DOE officials, the current Hawai'i State Teachers Association (HSTA) President, and Hawai'i state government officials, including state legislators, discuss their programs in detail. For a former professional dancer and singer on Broadway, this seemed a strange fit for Cheri, but as she spoke at meetings, I realized that her previous stage presence and her acumen as a former stockbroker who spoke fluent Japanese made her a person with the right skill set to host meetings and to deliver the critical question when it was necessary. I learned a great deal at HE'E meetings. Cheri would often come to PUEO events, as this Partnership was a two-way street. This was an easy Partnership; it turned into a Marriage with regular visits at Starbucks and many, many discussions about educational philosophy as it applied to the Hawai'i State Department of Education. Cheri's information was critical for the director of PUEO.

All of our P-M relationships made the road to success in the PUEO program so much easier. I always felt/feel so indebted to the generous and warm-hearted people mentioned above, and especially to all those in the Hawai'i DOE.

CHAPTER VII

How Does One Get High School Kids into College? (The College P-M Model)

The marriage with Dr. Amy Agbayani, mentioned earlier (and now nationally known on television as Amy represented Hawai'i at the Democratic National Convention 2020 roll call vote, with Diamond Head and Waikiki Beach as her backdrop), at the University of Hawai'i was followed, after she retired from UH, by a Partnership with Dean Denise Konan of the Social Sciences Department, Professor Dick Pratt, and with the noted business leader Robbie Alm. But first, a brief shout-out to our hardworking college counselors in PUEO.

Mr. Dan Feldhaus, the former Iolani College counselor, was semi-retired—but not really.

My first recollection of this tall, midwestern Yale graduate was one weekend where the rest of us at Iolani (before Punahou and PUEO) were relaxing and doing the normal weekend things. I had the fortunate opportunity to go to the Feldhaus abode in Hawai'i Kai for some academic reason or another. Inviting me in was the former administrative assistant to Headmaster David Coon, the fast-talking, most gregarious, and warm Joyce Feldhaus, Dan's wife. She had once put me on hold when I was calling from the Bay Area just after the Bay Bridge earthquake and hundreds of people were in line for a single telephone booth (a time with no cell phones). I never let her live this down, as her daughter Lara, a favorite student of mine at Iolani, was about to visit us and I was trying to discourage Lara from coming to Berkeley after this damaging earthquake. Well, Joyce did not know about the earthquake, but this didn't stop me from annoying her with this story. Back to Dan. When I walked in the front door, there was Dan sitting on the carpeted floor with literally every part of the carpet covered with files of students who were applying to college. "Hardworking" doesn't really cover it with this Iolani administrator. So when I asked Dan to be our first college counselor, his "yes" was more than joyful.

Dan Feldhaus would act as a college counselor for the seventh and final year of our initial cohort of PUEO students coming to Punahou for classes. The first year this happened, the first year, that is, that we needed a college counselor, was 2011. Depending on the year and the availability of classrooms, Dan would team up with the wonderful Dayna Kaneshiro (Roosevelt High School counselor) to produce a better-than-excellent college counseling program. In this summer class students would get the ABCs of applying to college before their senior year of high school. They would be asked to present their favorite college to the P7 group, giving various metrics, sharing geographical location, and so on. During their senior year, Dan would follow up with his former summer students by touching base with these students ten times by group meetings at specific high schools or by inviting students into his private office, which was a stone's throw from the Punahou campus. This routine was followed by Dan's successor, Mr. Curtis Nishioka, formerly the lead admissions director at University of Hawai'i, Hilo. And in turn, Curtis would mentor his successor, the wonderfully young and energetic college counselor Adrian Kerwin (son of the magic supervisor and critical administrator, Dr. Brad Kerwin).

Paired with our College P7 Program during the summers was generally a for-credit English class taught for many years by the wonderful Dr. Jeanette Hall. She was joined by another English teacher (in the most recent years Jillian Oyama from Kaiser High School) and as the program matured we formed a Partnership and then Marriage with the Mānoa Academy at the University of Hawai'i to get college credit for our PUEO Scholars through the previously mentioned Dean Konan and initially set up by Professor Dick Pratt. So our preseniors in high school were already getting college credit; what is more, Dick arranged for leadership expert and noted businessperson Robbie Alm to teach our PUEO students just before they entered college a year later, and so, in a sense, for a small PUEO group of fifteen students, we had an unofficial ninth year of PUEO. Some of these students were even afforded a University of Hawai'i trip to China by Dean Konan. Again, a strong Partnership and then Marriage as this developed over several years with the Mānoa Academy at the University of Hawai'i.

Now a description of the college trip from the island of O'ahu to the Big Island of Hawai'i must be elucidated as it was so much a part of the successful conclusion for our students. During their high school senior year, either in September or October, we would meet our P7 students who had graduated from the academic classes at PUEO the previous summer, at the Honolulu Airport around 4:30–5:00 a.m. We would hurry the students into the airport with their identification cards, hand out about fifty tickets, and get them on a plane to the Big Island, where they would be greeted at the Hilo Airport by a rented bus that would serve as our transportation home until about 8:00 p.m. After making sure we had all on the bus accompanied by at least five or six of their *kumu* (an accounting we always did on all field trips), we ventured to Ken's House of Pancakes, the noted Hilo place for pancakes, Portuguese sausage, and eggs.

This was another example of our Partnership-Marriage formula, applied to a restaurant. We began by initiating this Partnership during our first visit with seniors in high school, and by the eighth year of entering Ken's Pancakes, they had a separate room for us and already knew our order (each child received eggs, pancakes, and a breakfast that also contained meat and fruit). After stomachs were full, we ventured to the University of Hawai'i at Hilo where we first would visit the Department of Hawaiian Studies (one of the few places where one can receive a PhD in Hawaiian language and culture). The department members always greeted us with a traditional Hawaiian greeting and chant, and we responded in Hawaiian under the longtime PUEO *kumu* Lisa Kamalani, who came each summer to O'ahu from her job teaching social studies at Waiakea High School in Hilo. We followed up this magnificent greeting with a brief introduction to UH Hilo by a respected member of their faculty, and this was followed by a tour of the department, where our students were able to see actual classes.

At the University of Hawai'i at Hilo, students were able to see a variety of classes from history to biology, from political science to astronomy. Our PUEO Scholars were taken around by an array of undergraduate students whose enthusiasm made all want to go to the University of Hawai'i at Hilo. Lunch took place in the UH Hilo Student Center, with an array of current undergraduates talking about their experiences at this very fine college. In later years of the program, PUEO students who attended UH Hilo would give us this tour and talk about UH Hilo at lunch.

After lunch, our students got back on the bus to take a field trip up to the Hawai'i Volcanoes National Park, about one hour up-country. When we stepped out of the bus, we traveled to the volcano museum and then to the site of an active part of the volcano, where we watched from the safety of the volcano park station that provided an amazing overview. Sometimes we saw the steam rising from the active Kilauea Caldera.

On the bus ride back to the university, students often slept before we landed at one of UH Hilo's cafeterias, where students ate heartily and filled out evaluations of this journey. PUEO students were also asked to focus on their college choices before we left on the bus for the airport. On our original trip to the Big Island, one of our students, Ariana, had wanted to stay to visit some family. As her family did not show up and the other students were waiting to get on the plane back to Honolulu, Lisa Kamalani, the Hawaiian studies teacher in PUEO who was based on the Big Island of Hawai'i, took her home after contacting Ariana's family for permission. Ariana was picked up by her family at Lisa's house much later. I mention this only because PUEO itself was akin to a family, and everyone always took care of one another.

Finally, around 10:00 p.m., the students and their chaperones made it back to O'ahu. Their parents picked up the sleepy kids, and the chaperones went home happy, realizing what they had done for these children this day. And for some of the PUEO Scholars (ages seventeen or eighteen), this was the first time they had been on a plane.

This wonderful trip was all possible because of the Partnership we had originally created with the admissions officer at UH Hilo, Mr. Curtis Nishioka. Our full Marriage with Curtis came when he became the college counselor after Dan Feldhaus retired. In addition, this trip would not have been possible without the coordination of the assistant director of PUEO, Mrs. Kylee Mar, who set up the visits with the Hawaiian Studies program at UH Hilo and the always kind and thoughtful Mrs. Seri Suzuki, who focused on the complicated logistics of each trip.

***

At the end of their senior year in high school and after they had graduated from the PUEO Program formal classes the year before, PUEO students were often invited to the majestic house sitting atop the Punahou campus, the home of President James Scott. Students were serenaded by speeches from PUEO graduates and members of the Clarence T. C. Ching Foundation. They were given scholarships by the Mamoru and Aiko Takitani Foundation, always represented by board members Jan Loo and Lynne Tsuda. Students ate and celebrated before they went off to college. Their PUEO journey was complete.

CHAPTER VIII

How Does One Find Support for the Program? (Donors Fitting the P-M Model)

When President James Scott, all those many seventeen years ago, asked me to start a Summerbridge-type program, he did ask me after a nice lunch at the Pacific Club (think fancy business club) to raise the money for the program, too. As I found out, this would not be a terribly difficult task, although at first it seemed daunting. The reason for the relative ease of donor relationships in PUEO came as a result of our locale and culture; in Hawai'i, you not only have generous donors, but these donors also tend to be humble, unassuming, and kind.

While working with Barbara Morgan of our Punahou Advancement Department, several donors immediately were encouraged and excited by the idea of PUEO. The Harry and Jeanette Weinberg Foundation had always been generous to the people of Hawai'i, largely donating buildings to institutions who served the poor and needy in Hawai'i and also to various Jewish affiliated groups—and sometimes a mixture of both. A lovely woman named Gailene Wong was in charge of the grant department at Weinberg, and she was so kind to offer seed money for PUEO. But this was not the first time we had begun to partner with Gailene and the Weinberg Foundation.

Shortly after President Scott came to Punahou School in the early 1990s, Gailene was trying to figure out a way to give students a further inducement to do community service and service-learning. She turned to Jim and me to get some advice regarding this type of motivation as we were both experienced educators. Jim set me to the task. While Gailene wanted to give small grants of $2,000 to nonprofits allowing students to complete about one hundred hours of work (collectively), she initially wanted the grant proposals to come from students. Knowing the sometimes scattered nature of most high school students and the fact that some will graduate and leave Hawai'i, I suggested an alternative: use teachers instead. Shortly after our conversation, Gailene would launch the Educating the Heart Program (words taken from Reverend John Heidel, the Punahou School chaplain, who talked about this in his sermons at Punahou). The Educating the Heart Program lasted for over two decades, and eventually Gailene raised the initial grant from $2,000 to $5,000, and through this process the Weinberg Foundation ended up giving more than several million dollars to local nonprofits in the Hawai'i community. Also, each student who worked in this service-learning Educating the Heart Program received a letter from the Harry and Jeanette Weinberg Foundation acknowledging their fine work. Many people associated with Youth Service Hawaii (mentioned earlier) took advantage of this opportunity offered by Gailene. The Partnership with Gailene Wong blossomed into a real Marriage when the Harry and Jeanette Weinberg Foundation not only helped launch PUEO, but also helped Punahou years before with the building of Weinberg Hall where our PUEO Program first housed its classes. One trustee of this foundation became a friend and also was part of this P-M relationship: Corbett Kalama. A tall, thoughtful, and generous man, Corbett is someone who always walks the walk. Our conversations most often revolve around what we can do for others. As a former trustee of the Kamehameha Schools in Hawai'i, this is a man who spends every waking hour devoted to the people of Hawai'i, and when he is not doing this work, he is a devoted family man.

One really never knew who would be interested in the PUEO Program. On one morning, I received a call from the friendly missionary descendent Barbara Morgan, who was working in development at Punahou. Apparently, a young couple was interested in PUEO, and they wanted to meet in the Lily Pond Room of our Luke Center for Public Service. Relatively central to the PUEO Program, as we meet adjacent to the Lily Pond for our morning Hawaiian chant (*oli*), the Lily Pond is a natural pool watered by our spring, Ka Punahou (hence the name of the school) on its mountain end (we say *mauka* in Hawai'i for going toward the mountains, *makai* for going toward the beach and ocean). Here lies our beautiful chapel, where the carp from the Lily Pond flow just below the chapel so that students a bit tired from services can sometimes see carp jumping or at least swishing the water around (in the back right-hand side of chapel as one is facing the cross). Adjacent to the chapel lies one of the most beautiful meeting rooms, with the Lily Pond in full view underneath a hala tree, which is a symbol of our Punahou School. As the hala tree, the Lily Pond, and Ka Punahou play into the minds of all at the school, the legend must be repeated here before we go on:

> **"The Legend of Ka Punahou"**
> *(taken from the USC Folklore Website)*
> A long time ago, there was a very dry time on the island of O'ahu. No rains fell. All the streams were dry. Because there was no rain, the crops were not able to grow and the people were becoming worried.
>
> At the foot of Rocky Hill at the base of Mānoa Valley lived an old couple and these dry times were hard on them...

Every day, Mukaka, the husband, would walk up to Mānoa Valley to get *ti* roots and ferns for food. His wife, Kealoha, would walk down to Ka-Mo'ili'ili where the stream flowed. She would fill her water gourds there and carry them up the long, rough trail to her home near Rocky Hill.

One day, the trip seemed more difficult than ever, so Kealoha stopped to rest on a rock. Water was very important, so she knew she needed to go to Ka-Mo'ili'ili each day. But she was very tired, and didn't want to continue.

She got up and lifted her carrying pole. It was a windy day, and the wind almost blew her down, but she struggled to walk back home. Mukaka was preparing food when she arrived home, but she was too tired to eat. She laid down on her mats and cried because she was so weary. When she finally got to sleep, she had a dream.

In the dream, a man stood by her and asked, "Why are you crying?"

Kealoha answered that she was very weary because of the long, hot, dusty path she had to take every day to Ka-Mo'ili'ili and that she was too tired.

The man told Kealoha that she didn't need to go to Ka-Mo'ili'ili every day because under a hala tree near her home there was a spring. And there she could fill her gourds. Then the man was gone. In the morning, Kealoha told Mukaka about her dream. But he didn't think it was true. He thought it was an empty dream that came about because she was thirsty.

Mukaka began to walk toward the upland *mauka*, and Kealoha watched him, wondering why he didn't do what the dream said: pull up the hala tree to search for the spring. She went to look at the tree and saw that the ground was dry and hard, so maybe there wasn't any water there. The dream *must* have been empty.

But that night as they were sleeping, Mukaka had a dream. In his dream, a man sat by him and told Mukaka that there *was* water under the tree. The man told Mukaka what to do. Mukaka had to catch some red fish, cook them in an *imu*, and then make an offering. Only *then* would Mukaka have the strength to pull the hala tree out of the ground to fill the spring.

When Mukaka got up the next morning, he realized he had the same dream as his wife; he knew he needed to do what the man in the dream said to do. So Mukaka and a friend went to Waikiki to fish. They were able to catch some red fish; Mukaka knew that the god Kāne was with them. They rushed home to heat the *imu*. When the fish were cooked, Mukaka prayed. Then they ate. And after that, Mukaka told his friend about the two dreams he and his wife had had. Now it was time to pull up the hala tree to see if there was any truth to the dream. The two men grabbed the hala tree, and they pulled hard. Their muscles strained, and sweat poured down their bodies. They stopped for a while, then tried again, but the tree didn't move. The friend looked at the ground and said that there couldn't be any water there.

Mukaka said that he *knew* the dream was true. He knew Kāne was with them. So he had to try again. So the two men began to pull again, and this time, the tree began to move. They pulled harder and harder, and, finally, the tree came out of the ground. And they saw water moistening the earth. Mukaka ran to get his *o'o* (digging stick) to clear away the dirt and stones. A tiny stream began to gush out. The three people stared, and Kealoha shouted, "*Ka Punahou*! The new spring!"

Now there was water for the entire neighborhood! Kealoha didn't have to walk to Ka-Mo'ili'ili. Water soaked the ground. Walls were built, and taro was planted. Through these *lo'i kalo* (taro patches), water flowed steadily. *I'a* (fish) were brought there. The *i'a* and *kalo* grew, so the spring provided food as well as water. The people thanked the gods of agriculture, Kāne and Lono. Now their lives were good.

Many years later, a school, Punahou, was built beside that spring. And it bears the name Kealoha shouted in joy. The school seal is a hala tree with water and *kalo* leaves. The founders of Punahou said that the school would be a spring for wisdom, a fountain of learning. As the hala tree stands firm through wind or storm, so shall the children of this school stand strong and brave through joy and sorrow. As the hala has many uses, so shall these children be useful to Hawai`i.

And so into the room of the Luke Center for Public Service with a view of the mythical and legendary Lily Pond in full view came these two young parents with a toddler and a baby; Barbara Morgan had invited them to talk to me about the PUEO Program at Punahou. Bill Reeves, the dad, has a happy demeanor and is quietly observant. His unassuming qualities mask the genius of a man who is a proud Yale graduate; Bill mastered his financial prowess in England and set up a lucrative business in Europe. His partner and wife, Debbie Berger, has the elegance and brilliance one would expect from this power couple—and it is she who has the *chutzpah* in the family. Reminding me of my own daughter with similar lineage (that is, Japanese and Jewish ancestry), Debbie does not mince her words. She is straightforward, kind, and full of ideas. In the past decade, she became a Punahou School trustee and is also a trustee of Smith College, and she most recently became the chair of the board of the Hawaii Community Foundation. Her incredible business background is also in finance and banking.

What is remarkable about these two special people is that they set up the initial funds for PUEO because they understood the significance of the program. They knew that students with limited resources might need help and guidance to get them into college. They knew that the playing field needed to be leveled. Meeting them in the Lily Pond Room of the Luke Center, a center devoted to service, with, as I mentioned, a beautiful view, seemed all the more appropriate. With their newly established Unbound Philanthropy nonprofit, they formed much of the seed money for PUEO, and I have always credited Debbie and Bill for helping to launch PUEO. As time progressed in the program, I would meet with this couple, sometimes at Town, one of their favorite restaurants in Honolulu. I was always impressed by their candor, their acute observations, and their continual kindness to this aging Ashkenazi man. This Partnership turned into a philosophical Marriage, as I often discussed educational ideas with this more than generous couple. Often, I would see them at various PUEO or Punahou events, and in the brief moments we would see each other, ideas would be exchanged.

Early in the program, the Harold K. L. Castle Foundation heavily supported the PUEO Program. Mitch D'Olier is a tall, gregarious, and thoughtful man. Mitch is currently the President and CEO at Kaneohe Ranch Management, LLC. "Thoughtful" and "friendly" describe this CEO and board member of the Harold K. L. Castle Foundation. Mitch early on understood, much like the Reeves-Berger couple, the significance of the PUEO Program, and when Punahou School delayed a bit in its building of a new building that had Castle monies earmarked for the project, with simple negotiations the money was transferred to PUEO instead. Mitch's protégé at the time, Terry George, who is now CEO of the Harold K.L. Castle Foundation, is one of those guys you meet in life who always has a kind word for everyone. These two men took a look at the PUEO Program and then supported it.

Mitch and Terry have supported other educational ventures including Teach for America and the Castle High School Redesign Movement, among so many more educational improvement ventures. Their hearts are always in the right place, and the donation to PUEO was in sync with their overall goals in life. My Partnership with Mitch went back to an educational conference in upstate New York. As I remember, Mitch was one of the keynote speakers at this College For Every Student Conference (CFES), and I would see Mitch at other CFES meetings. In fact, for over fifteen years I have seen Mitch and Terry at various functions; the Harold K. L. Castle Foundation has had a laser focus on improving the educational institutions for children, especially on the windward side of O'ahu. I remember meeting with Terry George at a café named Sure Shot near the Punahou School campus. Terry would drive his Prius there after dropping off his kids at Punahou. His demeanor was friendly, his eyes were always filled with joy, and the conversation about serious issues facing education in Hawai'i was upbeat and purposeful.

My initial Partnership with Mitch was created when he and his lovely wife, Bambi, were talking about Claremont-McKenna College, where their son had attended college. My oldest daughter, Laura (now Professor Laura Keiko Gilah Ackerman at Arizona State University), eventually attended this same extraordinary college. Ironically, other very helpful PUEO donors with their HOEA Foundation, Eric and Lori Fujimoto, were also great advocates for Claremont-McKenna. The professors at Claremont-McKenna set my daughter in the direction of chemistry, where she remains today. Terry and I had conversations over several years about the Castle High School complex in Hawai'i, and we marveled how Dr. Marlene Zeug led those meetings. Indeed, these meetings, often in the rural-based KEY Project in Kahalu'u, really engaged the community about educational pursuits. It was always a pleasure to see Terry and Mitch because the two gentlemen were committed to the children of Hawai'i. The Partnership and eventual deep Marriage relationship I have had with Mitch and Terry came through multiple meetings and conversations over many years.

The most generous and sustaining support for the Clarence T. C. Ching PUEO Program at Punahou School came from the foundation that is now carried in our official name: the Clarence T. C. Ching Foundation. Current members of this board are Jack Tsui, Robert (Bob) Fujioka, Raymond (Ray) Tam, Ken Okamoto, and Catherine (Cathy) Ching (in addition to Peter Ng before his passing), with Tertia Freas (formerly Steve Gilley, who was a CEO of many businesses in his own right) serving as the executive director and Linda FitzGerald as the executive assistant. This single foundation has sustained the PUEO Program, and its members have fully supported all of our endeavors—a truly remarkable group of people.

It would be prudent to talk about Clarence T. C. Ching himself before one discusses this marvelous board. Clarence T. C. Ching was a Hawai'i rags-to-riches story, and his was the story of many who reached these islands as workers and then built their fortunes through one or two generations of incredibly hard work. Here is a brief explanation taken from the foundation's website of this Hawai'i-based American dream story:

Clarence, his wife Dorothy, and his 3 children, Wallace, Jocelyn and Lawrence

Clarence Thing Chock Ching was born on June 2, 1912, in Anahola, a scenic plantation village on the North Shore of Kauai. He was the fifth of eleven children born to Chinese immigrants Ching Koon Hook and Kam Sing.

Seeking a better life for their children, Ching Hook and Kam Sing relocated the family to Honolulu. Clarence enrolled at Saint Louis School, a private Catholic Marianist school founded in 1846. He excelled both in and out of the classroom. He was twice elected class president and became a member of the school's Chinese Literacy Improvement Association, an honor bestowed to students earning a scholastic average of 85 percent or higher. And although he was frail and sickly as a child, Clarence developed his body and endurance to become a champion boxer in high school.

Upon graduating from Saint Louis in 1932, Clarence attended night school and studied real estate and insurance. He married Dorothy Sau Pung Tom, with whom he had three children: Lawrence, Wallace, and Jocelyn. By the late 1930s, he was managing the family store at

Damon Tract, a residential and agricultural area next to what is now known as the Honolulu International Airport. He also began dabbling in real estate.

In 1956, Clarence and his business partner purchased 233 acres of Damon Tract. Less than a year later, the land was rezoned for airport and industrial use. Together, they developed Damon Tract into the Airport Industrial Park.

More success followed. Testing the waters of Hawai'i's low-cost housing market, Clarence built an ambitious housing development in Moanalua, which led to the developments in the Fort Shafter, Tripler, Red Hill, Moanalua Valley, and Salt Lake areas. In 1958, he began development of an area in Salt Lake that would eventually open as the Honolulu Country Club. Two years later, he was part of a group that founded Hawai'i National Bank. In the 1960s, in tribute to his Chinese heritage, Clarence played an instrumental role in the redevelopment of Chinatown Honolulu in the form of the Chinese Cultural Plaza. The pride and joy of his professional career, however, was developing Kukui Gardens, an 822-unit apartment complex for low-income residents.

Said his nephew, Raymond Tam: "The best part about Kukui Gardens? He donated all the money from the project to charity through his foundation. That is just the kind of person he was. He did not make a dime from Kukui Gardens. How many other successful businessmen would undertake such a project? His generosity and caring for the community made him special."

Clarence T.C. Ching died on May 29, 1985, at the age of 72. Just days after his passing, the *Honolulu Advertiser* wrote: "As the son of an immigrant father, Clarence Ching worked hard all his life. He proved that a humble beginning is no barrier if one has constructive dreams and the ability and determination to make them come true. His good deeds will live after him. But he will be sorely missed by all who knew him and of his deep care for the community."

It was this legacy that produced the Clarence T. C. Ching PUEO Program at Punahou School. All of the trustees of this foundation embody the kindness, generosity, and humble spirit of Clarence T. C. Ching. The chair of the board, Jack Tsui, has the demeanor of a scholar and was a man I carefully listened to in all our meetings. "A straight shooter," as my stepfather Jerry Shore would have said, and his gentle way of asking about the program always impressed me. "How are things going?" Jack would say as he greeted me at different events. Cathy Ching is the quiet, charming trustee who quietly asks penetrating questions and shows up at many of our events. Cathy took the time to visit the program on many occasions, and often I saw her smiling at our events; she also took the time to talk to the kids.

Bob Fujioka is the man you want to talk to on any occasion—sincere, friendly, and a man who just seems to radiate life. A simply delightful person. Ray Tam is a man I have admired for many years. He is taciturn but has a "heart of gold" (to borrow from a Neil Young song). During one of our first encounters with Ray, he asked, "So, how are you spending our money?" I thought it was a fair question and, in Mr. Tam's general framework, direct. Peter Ng, before his unfortunate passing, was another quiet trustee. He would approach me during events, speak softly, and ask acute questions about the PUEO children. This was a man who had faced adversity and seemed to always be aware of how others were feeling. Steve Gilley often had a fine question for me over the telephone and would discuss philosophical issues with me. One day we were talking about one of his sons who had done well in business, and I said, "What great luck, Steve." Steve replied, "You can't imagine how lucky people can be if they work really hard."

I will take this adage to the grave. Tertia Freas is a woman who worked for an international accounting firm and rose to its highest echelons. Straightforward, thoughtful, and precise—this is a woman you want leading your company. Linda FitzGerald, Tertia's assistant, greets all at the foundation with a smile and a warm greeting. It was she that made all of our gatherings filled with delicious food and warm ambiance.

And then there was my friend Ken Okamoto. I don't think I have ever seen Ken mad, upset, or troubled. He is a man full of grace, wit, and, from what I have been told (as I have never been in court with him), is a first-class trial lawyer. It is to Ken that we first broached ideas about the program. I remember sitting in one of our local chain restaurants in Hawai'i called Zippy's and asking Ken about the possibilities for further support for PUEO; he said he would take this idea to the other trustees.

In business, it is always great when you have someone you can always count on and whose word is really a bond. Ken represented the bond that initially put PUEO into a Partnership with all the trustees of the Clarence T. C. Ching Foundation. The Marriage was complete quite early in our relationship, and I considered my relationship with this foundation a sacred trust. When this most generous foundation gave us six million dollars at the president's lovely house at Punahou, the largest foundation gift in Punahou's history, several people spoke—Governor Ige was one of them. When Ken got up to speak about the children in PUEO (remember Ken is a tough, seasoned lawyer, despite his gentlemanly demeanor in social situations, with a kind smile and laugh), he had to stop as tears were running down his face. He then took a moment to compose himself. It was at that moment that I knew how deeply Ken and his fellow trustees felt about PUEO. While I am not a man prone to religious statements, I do believe there is a time and place for everything: God bless the Clarence T. C. Ching Foundation.

Other truly remarkable people have contributed to PUEO's support: the very talented entrepreneur Wally Tsuha; the most gregarious and prolific email writer and historian of England, Peter Hoffenberg, through his Sidney Stern Memorial Trust; Michele Morikami, a woman who set up the wonderful accounts in PUEO; and the Ackerman family. The Reverend Abraham Kahu Akaka Ministries Foundation gave a special scholarship to those PUEO students who had a strong relationship with religion; the granddaughter of Reverend Abraham Akaka (who was a celebrated Hawaiian minister who gave Dr. Martin Luther King, Jr. his lei for his march in Selma), graced us with her kumu prowess as our first PUEO intern. And I am only mentioning the generosity of those who I can remember using the aging synapses of a mind well into its sixties. All our donors began as partners and were married to the program fairly quickly. All who visited PUEO understood its mission and its proven success. This is what turned Partnership into Marriage with our donors.

CHAPTER IX

Why Go to Conferences? (NSLA, NPEA, and NPLC Conferences and P-M)

When PUEO first started, my friend Milton Chen, Director of the George Lucas Educational Foundation at the time, told me about an organization called the National Summer Learning Association. I remember reading about it during the time in PUEO when we had only forty Scholars and my office was located in the new (at that time) Mamiya Science Building at Punahou School. During our huge Punahou Carnival (one really should google this large affair that takes over our entire campus during the first weekend in February), I had retreated to my office to help fill out an application for their national award for excellence in summer learning. While we did not win that year, we would win years later. In the meantime, we attended NSLA religiously for many years, crisscrossing across the country, as NSLA would pick different cities for their conferences: Baltimore, Atlanta, Washington, DC, San Francisco, and the list goes on. We heard everything---from new types of classes during the summer to an array of issues that made truly excellent learning during the summer so important.

The president of the board and founder of NSLA was Matthew Boulay (who is still there today). The remarkable thing about Matthew is that his educational career seems to have started in the Marine Corps, and he started

NSLA as a student at Johns Hopkins University. His CEO at the time was Ron Fairchild, another gregarious, charming, and dedicated person in education. We started going (Brad Kerwin, Kylee Mar, Suzanne Sato, and others) to NSLA early during its existence. The workshops were always instructive, the keynotes informative, and the technical accumulation of data—which makes programs so much easier to function and thrive—was simply astounding. We often gave our own workshops (designed by Brad, myself or others) about PUEO at NSLA and other conferences, too. Our name became well known nationally because of these workshops.

For one of our best P-M relationships, in walked Brenda McLaughlin from NSLA. Brenda, sharp as a tack and always upbeat, is one of those people who never ages. She offered us her managerial services (in her role as an administrator/consultant for NSLA) in producing a longitudinal study. Surveys, interviews, and observational visits by Brenda and her crew helped us deliver the first PUEO longitudinal study. This study helped us by giving statistical information to our donors (remember it took us eight years to get our first students to go from sixth grade, graduate from high school, and then go to college) and by letting us know how PUEO as a program was doing. Brenda asked the right questions. Matthew Boulay, who I consider a friend to this day, always made us feel comfortable at the NSLA conferences. Matthew was able to personally observe PUEO when he left his Seattle abode (even though NSLA was located in Baltimore) and spent about a week with us in Honolulu. He was suitably impressed with PUEO—we did receive his organization's award for excellence.

To make Partnerships, I always considered it necessary to learn about other organizations and what was being done nationally and sometimes internationally. It was important for others in PUEO, especially those in leadership positions, to see and hear how others did their job. The original Partnerships with Matthew and Brenda turned into true friendships and eventually our metaphor for the strongest business Partnership, the Marriage.

These conferences provided the bonding time so necessary for family and friends, too. I was struck by how the CEO, Ron Fairchild, one night after a hard day's work at NSLA took his children to a Chicago Cubs' game. When in Baltimore, John Reppun, Brad Kerwin, and I took in an Orioles night game, and on that evening in Camden Yards, we watched Manny Machado hit a grand slam for the Orioles. While John and Brad were already in the Marriage category with the PUEO Program, I felt it was important to always take critical administrators and staff with me to these conferences to keep the glue that kept these Marriage relationships strong. My administrative staff and faculty often provided ideas about improving the PUEO Program after attending such conferences. Our awards from different organizations were often celebrated collectively with some of our key partners.

2016 Summer Learning Award from NSLA being celebrated in Hawai'i. Punahou PUEO staff shared the award with outgoing DOE Superintendent Kathryn Matayoshi in a DOE Board meeting in Honolulu. From left: Punahou Director of Foundation Relations Suzanne Sato, DOE Director of Community Engagement Marlene Zeug, PUEO Director Carl Ackerman, PUEO Administrative Assistant Sereny Suzuki, President Jim Scott, DOE Superintendent Kathryn Matayoshi, DOE Board Chair Lance Mizumoto, and PUEO Assistant Director Kylee Mar.

The National Partnership for Educational Access is another organization we found indispensable for our continued education in the Clarence T. C. Ching PUEO Program. The brainchild of the late Michael Danziger of the Steppingstone Foundation, led by Karin Elliott, this organization was simply set on providing more access to underserved students across the country. Much like NSLA, this wonderful organization, which started about the same time as PUEO in 2005, was a place to go for ideas, possible research about students who might be the first in their families to go to college, and to network with organizations doing the same work as PUEO. One such organization was the Prep@Pingree Organization (Now the Malcom Coates Prep@ Pingree Program) at the Pingree School just outside of Boston. Led by the gregarious, friendly, witty, and charming man, Steve Filosa, this program paralleled PUEO in many ways.

Steve was such a delightful person, and he invited me out to his school, Pingree, and I had a chance to get a feel for his program. As a late afternoon activity, Steve took me to a beach near his home, as he is an avid sailor. He said to me as a resident of Ipswich, Massachusetts, "Carl, have you ever seen such a beautiful beach?" Clearly, he had forgotten I was from Honolulu. Still, NPEA afforded networking possibilities beyond the pale, and Steve Filosa was a Partnership-Marriage figure worth his weight in gold (perhaps even more, as he is a pretty thin guy).

As I had mentioned about NSLA, NPEA also gave out an excellence award. I include this award just below. It was important for the Clarence T. C. Ching PUEO Program to be recognized both nationally and locally (our Hawai'i Department of Education had recognized us, too). This gave credence to what we were doing and let others know about our efforts. Here is the award announcement from the NPEA website and a picture of the two PUEO representatives sent to accept the award:

"PUEO's stability over the past twelve years is due in part to very generous support from the program's namesake, the Clarence T.C. Ching Foundation, along with founding and sustaining grants from other foundations and individuals. PUEO began with just forty students from thirteen public schools and now serves more than three hundred students in grades 6–12 from all over Hawai'i and has had an important impact on graduation and college acceptance rates for those students. Through this seven-year program—students typically enter in sixth grade and leave upon graduation from high school—students are immersed in educational summer school courses, small group mentoring classes, and group activities throughout the school year and see a 99 percent high school graduation rate as compared to an 80 percent national rate and an 82 percent rate for Hawai'i. Moreover, 84 percent of PUEO graduates go on to college as compared to a state average of 63 percent for Hawai'i's Department of Education students. This remarkable level of success comes from the program's design, which ushers students through their formative middle and high school years, engaging them with interactive summer classes in basic engineering, marine biology, Hawaiian culture, and even magic, coupled with group activities throughout the traditional academic year."

"2015 Award Recipient: The Clarence T.C. Ching PUEO Program at Punahou School. NPEA is pleased to announce the winner of the 2015 Award for Excellence in Collaboration—The Clarence T. C. Ching PUEO Program at Punahou School. Brad Kerwin (Coordinator) and Suzanne Sato (Advancement, Leadership Giving Officer) of PUEO received the award at the NPEA 2015 conference on April 16th. The PUEO Program identifies students at neighboring public middle and high schools and aims to raise these students' aspirations and preparation to thrive in college by utilizing resources at Punahou School for a seven-year educational experience that includes summer school classes, small group mentoring, and academic-year group activities."

Pictured (left to right): *NPEA Advisory Board member John Leach (Director of Financial Aid, Emory University), Award for Excellence in Collaboration winners Brad Kerwin (Coordinator, PUEO Program) and Suzanne Sato (Advancement, Leadership Giving Officer, PUEO Program), and NPEA Planning Committee member Kamper Floyd (Director, Jackson* Get2College *Center, Education Services Foundation)*

About seven or eight years ago, Maureen Dowling, a critical administrator in the National Department of Education, invited President Jim Scott and me to a meeting at the LBJ Building at the National Department of Education—this was the National Private Leadership Conference. Maureen is savvy, sensationally kind to all, and knows all at the conference, always approaching with a typical warm handshake and an address by one's first name. The National Department of Education has a branch dedicated to private educators (a bit surprising, I know); at this annual conference, religious schools of every denomination, homeschoolers, lawyers advocating for private schools, and a couple of independent schools, among others, gathered to hear various items that concerned private education in the United States. A few public school district officials attended also. What made this conference special was that it consisted of only several hundred people, and often the Secretary of Education would speak and mingle. Secretary Arne Duncan sat on panel that included private school heads Jim Scott and Al Adams. The current Secretary of Education, Betsy DeVos, has addressed this small gathering for the last couple of years. It has been an honor to be invited by Maureen to this gathering for many years now—and our Partnership has cemented into a Marriage by many invitations—as this conference is invitation only. Any educational institution like PUEO must make these sorts of P-M relationships if they are to be successful on both a local and national level.

Of course, we attended other conferences, and I sent others to these conferences, too. This included organizations with an array of purposes, as in the College Board, where we received two other national awards, an array of organizations that dealt with college counseling, and local groups that worked on important native Hawaiian issues. The purposes of these trips all played into the overall idea of enhancing the visibility, the culture, and the camaraderie of the Clarence T. C. Ching PUEO Program.

CHAPTER X

How Does One Build a National Model of P-M? (PSPP)

The former Director of the George Lucas Educational Foundation (GLEF), Dr. Milton Chen, a six-foot, impeccably dressed man who would fit easily on the front page of any glamour magazine and who speaks in soft tones with a smile that makes you know that this is one brilliant guy, was one of our first evaluators of the PUEO Program. Each year I would invite two distinguished educators, from Milton to professor of French history at Wesleyan College Oliver W. Holmes, from Professor Ray Hebert, another historian turned administrator (much like the evaluator from Texas, Dean Jeffrey Hamilton) to the actress Dinah Manoff, to take a look at and to evaluate the PUEO Program. Beth Casey from the Middle School Partnerships (much like PUEO) came in from Baltimore, and Jenny Cousins and Carl Warner left their museum life in England and crossed two ponds, the Atlantic and the Pacific, to come and observe PUEO; Professor Diana Solomon only had to cross one pond from her college in Vancouver, Canada, to come and take a look at our English classes. This was simply a way for me to get a respected, international view of the Clarence T. C. Ching PUEO Program. One evaluator, a fellow history teacher from New Jersey, Tony Maccarella, had everyone charmed in PUEO with his quite distinctive "Jersey" accent. All loved Mr.

Maccarella. There was also the sage advice from Nicholas Chiorian—one of Cleveland's finest teachers—and from Theresa Jespersen, an administrator from Atlanta, along with her friend from Seattle, Jamie Oleson. Dr. James H. Carter, the Superintendent of the Selma School District in Alabama gave us his careful and wise inspection. We had the distinguished Reverend Olivia Hilton from Washington, DC, look at PUEO, too.

Gerard Robinson was a revered evaluator as he worked as the lead educator in several states and then worked with historically black colleges and universities; he is now the Vice-President for Education at the Advanced Studies in Culture Foundation at the University of Virginia. By the time I left PUEO, we had fifteen years of evaluators coming into PUEO. One of my precious gifts to the incoming administration of PUEO and to the new sage president of Punahou School, Professor Michael Latham, was a booklet comprised of these evaluations. A key to success in any organization is to listen what others are saying—and to bravely accept all constructive criticism.

Milton made critical observations of PUEO, as did all the evaluators, but his invitation to come and visit him at the Skywalker Ranch in Marin County is really what led to Private Schools with Public Purpose (PSPP). This was an amazing opportunity, and Milton hosted me at this George Lucas "Ranch" in Marin County near San Francisco; I stayed at a type of host lodging there, complete with kitchen facilities and very large rooms named after key directors or other Hollywood folk. As I recall I was in the Orson Welles Room. Not too far away was a softball field and a winery on this huge Marin estate.

Well, at this educational summit, George Lucas serenaded us with wonderful new ideas about education and showed us clips of his newest films. I repeatedly was asked if I was married to (at that time) the San Francisco superintendent of education whose last name was Ackerman also. Nope. I so enjoyed this time at this glorious Marin abode, meeting

CEOs of different tech companies who were staying with me at the "Lucas Lodge" and having some quality time with Milton. This quality time included a conversation about the start-up of PUEO. I told Milton how helpful people like Barbara Gee, Alec Lee (Aim High), and T.J. Vassar had been in my original ideas and in the launching of the PUEO Program as P-M colleagues. Milton, always being an idea man, suggested that we duplicate this type of kindness with an institutional structure—hence the birth of the concept of Private Schools with Public Purpose (PSPP).

So PSPP was launched within a year by inviting a select group of people to the George Lucas Headquarters in the Presidio in San Francisco. Barbara Gee was there from Head-Royce School in Oakland, M.J. Thorne from the Westminster School in Atlanta, T. J. Vassar and family came from LEEP in Seattle, a representative came from the Kamehameha School System in Honolulu, and others also attended. It was a small group, but we decided to have an organization that would help other schools get started in programs like Heads Up, LEEP, etc., and we would meet yearly to share ideas. We also thought we might always meet at a host school, and it was Barbara Gee (so typical of this generous woman) who volunteered first. As an aside, Milton, the busy GLEF director, would drop in on us from time to time at this "creation" meeting of PSPP just to make sure everything was going okay. Everyone at this initial meeting close to the San Francisco Bay was a dreamer, and we collectively put PSPP together through the bonds we already had in our Partnership-Marriage system.

Barbara Gee and I, for most of the life of PSPP, acted as codirectors, although now we have handed off the reins to younger people. Our Marriage relationship served us well, and I will simply discuss some of the highlights of the twelve PSPP conferences, ranging from 2005 to the present day. Our next one is scheduled for after the coronavirus in 2021 in Pasadena under the supervision of one of the new PSPP directors, Jose Melgoza at the Polytechnic School in Pasadena, California.

The Lakeside School in Seattle served PSPP twice under the quite strong leadership of Latasia Lanier, getting some help, as I recall, from Willie Adams (another new PSPP director) from Head-Royce during the second visit of PSPP to this school. Not only did participants get workshops about setting up private-public Partnerships, but also workshops on service-learning, philanthropic efforts as a part of this private-public process, and many other educational issues that dealt with Partnerships. And this was the rule for many of our PSPP gatherings. What gave these conferences such a meaningful culture was they were set at schools where children were ever-present. Conference fees were kept low, as our goal was to just break even or to make a little money to pass to the next conference. This set up an institutional Partnership-Marriage system whereby the promoters of the conference at one school would hand money and advice on to their future partner as one PSPP conference ended and another school took over the planning for the subsequent meeting. As the conference became imminent, that Partnership turned into a Marriage as the advice about things like registration, cost of food, and placement of workshops became the subject of lengthy and worthwhile discussions (perhaps we can call this educational family planning).

At each location, a preconference event would take place, and in Seattle it was at the Melinda & Bill Gates Foundation. All of our teachers and students made their way to this location and really learned about things that were offered by this visionary foundation. Latasia made sure we ate the wonderful food of the Lakeside Cafeteria and that we were able to interact with donors that made her program possible (critical shared resources). What we all most appreciated during one of our early meetings at the Lakeside School was seeing the students present information about themselves, which was duplicating what students did in the summer in LEEP in the activity called Stand and Deliver. An invention of the late T. J. Vassar, students would stand and deliver a speech about themselves or about their interests (as mentioned earlier). This was an exercise that not only promoted public, articulate, speech, but also gave students greater confidence. Often we would have wonderful guest speakers, as in the Jesuit President of Seattle University, Father Stephen Sundborg, who gave us a philosophical approach to the work we were doing. It was my pleasure to be able to greet Father Sundborg at the Seattle PSPP and to have a discussion with him about the Jesuit philosophy about our work.

Father Stephen Sundborg, President, Seattle University, at PSPP with the author.

Barbara Gee hosted at Head-Royce School in Oakland—twice. In the latter PSPP conference, she partnered with several schools in San Francisco. In one of the preconference activities, we worked in a soup kitchen at a church in San Francisco—a very moving experience to say the least. Passing students as we went to our workshops was always a pleasure at our two conferences at Head-Royce. As the food sometimes had to be delivered to the PSPP partner schools in San Francisco for our lunches and other meals, we needed to drive a truck across the Bay Bridge to deliver the food—my job. These were very much hand-on activities, and they kept our costs down. In another PSPP conference at Al Adams's Lick-Wilmerding School near the outskirts of San Francisco touching on City College, we witnessed new buildings in their first stages, and we had a party at what looked like a newly designed Gap Center in San Francisco; we were able to walk to San Francisco City College from this marvelous venue. Al Adams, longtime head at Lick, had encouraged one of his teachers, Alec Lee, to develop what will become a national organization called AIM High. Alec's work in creating and sustaining Aim High has simply been unfathomable; he was a mentor to me along with Al Adams as we created PUEO.

In Cleveland, Ohio, at the all-girls Hathaway Brown School (in the Shaker Heights part of Cleveland), we heard about youth philanthropy boards for students and how the school provided funds for students to give money away to appropriate nonprofits. Students were learning the skills of planned philanthropy. In Cleveland, there was an excursion to several museums and even to the Rock and Roll Hall of Fame. Camille Seals was our exquisite host at the Hathaway Brown School under the direction of Headmaster Bill Christ; all participants were bused from a nearby Marriott. It was so nice seeing the girls at this school working diligently as we attended this PSPP.

In Washington, DC, under Catherine Pearson's leadership at the Georgetown Day School, we had service-learning workshops and a keynote session by an entrepreneur who made a fortune in selling tea. Catherine left our presence suddenly to go and coach her school's tennis team. We intentionally wanted to make PSPP function within the borders of living schools. I remember distinctly how one student was talking to his friend about his upcoming bar mitzvah when I was entering GDS in Washington, DC. The heads of schools were always some of our biggest supporters, and this was definitely true in Washington, DC. Russell Shaw, the head of school at GDS, was such an affable man who could fit in anywhere, but once you met him, you knew that his critical attention was on kids. As this was our tenth PSPP, we even celebrated with a cake at the end of our conference.

At the Spence School a year or so later on the Upper East Side of New York City, Danielle Passno hosted us in a school that ran vertically in its operational framework. The elevator determined where you were and which classes took place; as you exited the elevator on any given floor, you entered a slightly different educational world. One of the most interesting sessions in New York was a head of school panel narrated by a delightful person who asked very challenging questions. The theme of the discourse was based on the following question:

What is your school or nonprofit doing to help the children in New York?

All of the heads did well with this question. Ellanor "Bodie" Brizendine talked about her school's outreach all over New York City. The head of school at Horace Mann School, Dr. Thomas M. Kelly, seemed to exude the public purpose of private schools. Situated in the Bronx, this man's school combines service with ethics and has established, since 2006, a Center for Community Values & Action. His presentation in particular moved most at this PSPP conference. A highlight of this PSPP was a speech by Geoffrey Canada about his Harlem's Children Zone. This is a man who, no matter what the odds, will not give up on a child. In his world there are no bad kids—just not enough people who will bleed day and night to make sure a child succeeds.

To give one a perspective of what went on at a typical PSPP, here is a brief blurb from Rebecca Hong, who, with Danielle, was instrumental in organizing PSPP 2019 at the Spence School:

> The 2019 PSPP conference theme is *Collaborating in the Service of Justice,* and we will focus on the intersections of equity and justice work in our schools, organizations, and communities. We have an exciting line-up of speakers and events, including former CEO and board member of Harlem Children's Zone's Geoffrey Canada; Harvard Graduate School of Education faculty director of Making Caring Common, Richard Weissbourd; critical service-learning proponent and scholar Tania Mitchell; a heads panel of independent, public, and charter school leaders from around the NYC area; along with purpose, civic engagement, equity, and service workshops from a number of dynamic educators, and more.

It was always such a pleasure to have nationally known speakers at our PSPP conference. As I have mentioned, Milton Chen, the CEO (emeritus now) of the George Lucas Educational Foundation has been part of our movement. We have had executives from all walks of life join us; in Hawai'i we had Matt Levi, an investigative reporter and leader in a martial arts program for youth in some of the most economically challenged parts of Honolulu, and David Rosenthal, the well known Bay Area lawyer who has been devoting much of his time to creating and developing the Richmond Scholars program in Richmond, California. We were so fortunate to get Geoffrey Canada to speak at our recent PSPP gathering in New York, and ironically, several weeks later my wife and I saw him speak again in Honolulu at a standing-room-only venue at our convention center. The picture below features Assistant Professor Laura Keiko Gilah Ackerman, her father, Geoffrey Canada, and Jose Oromi, a national leader from the Horizons Program, just after Mr. Canada spoke to our group in New York.

Our PSPP conferences in Honolulu included Punahou, Iolani, DOE schools, and others. People stayed along the Waikiki Beach at the New Otani hotel, and the workshops included not only private-public Partnerships, but also information about the indigenous Hawaiian culture and also the growing of taro on the windward side of O'ahu. Participants actually experienced the traditional Hawaiian way of fishing at He'eia Fishpond. One of the moments I will always remember was when we had lunch at President Jim Scott's house, Hawaiian music playing in the background, and several local women spontaneously dancing hula. In our second PSPP conference in Hawai'i, we heard from the accomplished lawyer, David Rosenthal (mentioned earlier), who had set up a charter school through many Partnerships in Richmond, California, and Matt Levi (mentioned earlier) gave an autobiographical speech that included wonderful information about his martial arts program. In the previous incarnation of PSPP in Hawai'i, we had heard from Blas Guerrero, a professor in the Chicano Studies Program at UC Berkeley.

All of these PSPP conferences took an enormous amount of work. In Honolulu, it kept Seri Suzuki and Kylee Mar (Punahou School), Allison Blakenship (Iolani School), and Collen Murakami and Marlene Zeug (DOE) very busy. John Reppun and his brothers also spent a great deal of time at KEY working out the details of the conference. Seri Suzuki in particular, who set up the graphics (which we still use today) and registration, was doing enormous work for several months. And this happened for every PSPP—volunteer work made the conferences—and again, they have always been set at schools with children participating at every conference. It should be pointed out that one head of school, especially when we had PSPP in Hawai'i, set up scholarships for teachers to attend PSPP, clearly understanding the full meaning of PSPP from its beginning as he had built a Horizons

Program (led by the most able Luis Perez) at the Harley School (with influential board member Conger Gable) in Rochester, New York. And then he built a city-wide coalition of like-minded groups and institutions. Dr. Tim Cottrell, Headmaster at Iolani School in Honolulu, was this generous and supportive Head.

The next Private Schools with Public Purpose Meeting in Pasadena, California, in 2021 at the Polytechnic School will be hosted by the tall, soft-spoken gentleman, Jose Melgoca, who runs a multi-school private-public Partnership at his southern California school. Like many of the leaders of these types of PUEO programs, Jose also teaches at Polytechnic. The initial relationships built in PSPP have now been handed down to a coalition of younger teachers and administrators who most ably run the organization. They now are building their own Partnership-Marriage relationships. And this is the way it should be done. New beginnings.

As a way to honor all the work that was completed for the PSPP conferences, I include one invitation that went out across the United States for the 2014 Conference in Honolulu, alluded to above.

Schools with Public Purpose
UNAHOU STREET . HONOLULU, HI 96822

oha PSPP Colleagues,

/e began planning for PSPP Hawai'i over a year ago. During this time we have made many iends and discovered the real power of Partnerships. We look to the next three days to ake even more. Please feel free at lunch and during our partnership sessions (at the end each day), to exchange cards, numbers, emails, etc. We believe that by partnering we n help improve our service to students. We are all here to make sure that our students ad healthy lives, have the opportunity to go to college, and develop the moral character keep them making good decisions throughout their lives. We also want them to develop rue Grit."

njoy the next three days! Take in the beauty and the cultural significance of the Lo'i Kalo aro paddies) and Loko I'a (Fish Pond). See how Windward Educators have succeeded, ven under the most difficult of circumstances, in taking advantage of outdoor learning enues for public and private sector students. Watch the magic of Dr. Brad Kerwin and the agical artistry of Mr. Dave Roberts. On Friday evening be sure to attend the screening of e locally produced film, O'la, a new documentary about health care in Hawai'i (Meet the bulous filmmaker---Matthew Nagato at Punahou School's Wo International Center at 6:30 M on Friday, March 7th). Enjoy our Keynote Speaker, David Rosenthal, and learn how one n make a miracle of a school come true; listen to Matt Levi discuss his martial arts ogram, and how he uses this program to develop moral character, and to provide holarships. Watch the children of the Hu'i YMCA, and then in the afternoon on Saturday ten to a panel of practical practitioners, and then for a real highlight, hear the words of r students.

e will feast on the food provided by our professional chef in residence, Ken, at the Key; e will dine at Punahou for breakfast and lunch at 'Iolani. Well fed, and well nourished by ot only the food, but the food for thought at our 7th Annual PSPP we will march onward, ith more partnerships, to Oakland next year.

ith the Warmest Aloha,

rbara Gee	John Reppun	Allison Ishii	Carl Ackerman
-Director	ED	Director	Co-Director
PP	Key Project	Sullivan Center	PSPP

CO-DIRECTORS

DR. CARL ACKERMAN

MS. BARBARA GEE

REGIONAL DIRECTORS

MS. M.J. THORNE

MR. TONY MACCARELLA

DR. BONNIE TRAYMORE

MS. ALLISON ISHII

DR. OLIVER W. HOLMES

EPILOGUE

Of course, the Clarence T. C. Ching PUEO Program at Punahou School continues on today but with different leadership and direction—and this is the way it should be; the Program is now in the expert hands of Director Kehaulani Kealoha-Scullion and Administrative Assistants Donna Hosoda and Myra Kaneko. The pages here only reflect my tenure in creating and managing the program from 2003 (when envisioning first began in a serious way, although the idea of the program goes back even several more years) until July 19, 2019. Also, in order for any individual program to be successful, you also need to have the Partnership-Marriage model occurring within your organization, too. I watched these Partnership-Marriages develop with teachers like Ka'eo Vasconcellos and Lisa Kamalani in our Hawaiian history program; Matt Nakamura and Tim Lucas did this in our study hall-counseling program called The Nest; I watched P1–2 Supervisor Alan Lum use the P-M methodology with an array of teachers and also with student TAs in the program as he took many PUEO Scholars on various fieldtrips. And our college counselor teams from Dana Kaneshiro at Roosevelt High School, the former sage college counselor at Iolani School Dan Feldhaus, and Colleen Inaba from McKinley High School (with both Curtis Nishioka and Adrian Kerwin) all had formed great Partnerships and Marriages based on their work with the senior high school students in Hawai'i and their schools. Our Partnership-Marriage with Punahou Cafeteria administrator Marcia Wright and our Partnership-Marriage relationship with the bus company

Roberts Hawaii all led to our many successes. While many of these relationships were not discussed in detail in this book, they were critically important for the Clarence T. C. Ching PUEO Program and were often developed by the people in the program itself. Each of these Partnerships and Marriages were based on close one-to-one relationships. One final Partnership-Marriage, was the one with Emeritus Punahou Dean, Tiger Tom Metcalf; not only did he work almost every PUEO Lu'au and give us all guidance as one of our first evaluators, he brought me in to Punahou School, 28 years ago, and gave me advice not just about PUEO, but about life in general. And to conclude with, the most important Partnership-Marriage relationships—the ones that existed/exist with my wife, Lyn (my daily advisor), and my daughters, Laura and Jennifer—proved/prove that all successful Partnerships-Marriages, by definition, begin at home.

But I am not finished quite yet. Earlier in this book, there was the story of the Maluyo brothers, and I thought it would be fitting that a student should end this book with his story:

Partnerships in Unlimited Educational Opportunities Program (PUEO) at Punahou
has had a direct impact on my life.

Who am I?

My name is Darren Maluyo-Gilman Jr., but I go by Mana. When I was young, my biological parents chose drugs and lived a different lifestyle instead of caring for me and my two younger brothers. However, I was blessed to have God send my Auntie Nita, sister of my biological father, to raise us. It wasn't easy for Auntie Nita to raise us. It was Auntie Nita and the three of us—me, Darryl, and Dezmen. I was four years old when Auntie Nita found us homeless in Wahiawa. She told my biological father that she would take care of us. I didn't realize that moment would change our lives forever. At the time, I couldn't speak. My language skills did not develop. Darryl was three and had some behavior issues, and Dezmen was two and was 100 percent deaf. Mingo had not been born yet. Throughout my elementary years, I struggled in school. I had to develop my speech, I was developmentally delayed, and I had such low self-confidence. Auntie Nita tried her best to raise me and my brothers.

I remember the day Dr. Carl Ackerman met with me and said, "Mana, I want to welcome you to the PUEO *'ohana*" (Hawaiian word for family). I was thirteen years old and attending Washington Intermediate School. I remember feeling really nervous. I wondered if I could handle the PUEO Program. I did not have the chance to start the program in my sixth grade year. I was recommended by my *kumu hula* Carolee Nishi in my eighth grade year. I was nervous the first day since everyone else knew each other from previous summers. I managed to make friends and got to know the program. As years went by, I have learned and benefited by many things: life skills, the importance of schooling, and setting an example for my brothers.

Life Skills

Each year at PUEO was full of skills and exposure to many careers. As a P3 (PUEO third year) student, I learned math, English, and magic. From that summer, I learned public speaking (magic) and developed an interest in math. P4 was about the modern history of Hawai'i; I learned about the history and the culture of Hawai'i. P5 was the class Participation in Democracy, learning about the history and the dynamics of the United States government. P6 was about ACT prep and performing arts, learning about the strategies when taking tests, and performing and acting. P7 was about more prep for college, enrolling in the University of Hawai'i at Mānoa as a possible choice for college, and applying for scholarships.

Importace of College and Getting Ahead

There is a shout at PUEO where either the *kumu* or Dr. Ackerman stand in front of the entire PUEO Program and shout, "WHAT GROUP ARE YOU IN?" We all answered, "PUEO!" Dr. A or other *kumu* would then ask, "WHERE ARE YOU GOING?" We all answered, "COLLEGE!" And in one final question, the *kumu* or Dr. A would ask, "WHAT ARE YOU GONNA DO?" We all yelled at the top of our lungs: "GRADUATE!" After hearing that, it always made me think about the future. Being a part of the PUEO *'ohana* made me realize the importance of education. I made it a lifetime goal to attend a college and graduate.

PUEO also gives the opportunity to every student to earn high school credits. This gave me the chance to get ahead and to have time to apply for a scholarship and to think about my future.

Setting an Example for my Younger Brothers

One of the greatest things PUEO has given me is the opportunity to start a legacy...with my own brothers. PUEO has given me the opportunity to gain confidence, improve my academics, and, most importantly, inspire my brothers to achieve greater things as well. Throughout my time in the PUEO program, I was constantly challenged, encouraged, and inspired to think outside of myself, pursue my goals, and be an active citizen in my community. There were times when my family went through some form of crisis. The faculty and staff were always there to encourage me to persevere and push through. There were times when I struggled academically. Faculty and staff were always there to assist and guide. Then there were times I just needed an ear that would listen to me. The PUEO *'ohana* was always there. I am grateful to now be in a situation where I can inspire, encourage, and guide my brothers.

Now...

I am currently nineteen years old. I spent a year at Southern Virginia University and decided to return home to Hawai'i. I am working on my core requirements at Kapiolani Community College. My goal is to attend the University of Hawai'i School of Medicine. My brother Darryl is eighteen and is currently working on finishing high school. Dezmen (age sixteen) and Mingo (age fourteen) currently attend McKinley High School, and they are both PUEO Scholars.

My Auntie Nita has always told me and my brothers that it took a village to raise us. I am simply grateful that the PUEO *'ohana* was and is still part of our village. At the beginning of this essay, I wrote "PUEO has had a direct impact on my life," and I was wrong: PUEO has had a direct impact on my family.

Auntie Nita and the Maluyo brothers after church

And so we end with one more look at the children of the Clarence T. C. Ching PUEO Program at Punahou, and by so doing, we celebrate the success of the Partnership-Marriage methodology.

Students in the Clarence T. C. Ching PUEO Program gathered at Thurston Twigg-Smith Auditorium at Punahou School

CPSIA information can be obtained
at www.ICGtesting.com
Printed in the USA
LVHW070858210821
695815LV00035B/1349